GOD FOUND ME IN THE PIT OF HELL,
BUT HE DIDN'T LEAVE ME THERE

# THE

# UNASHAMED

# LIFE

# MIRIAH TAVERNA

*This book is dedicated to all those who long to love and be loved. And to Jesus, the Lover of my soul, who meets us where we are, but doesn't leave us where He finds us.*

# CONTENTS

Foreword ........................................................ vii
Preface ........................................................... x

1. The Choice Is Yours ...................................... 1
2. Born Into Sin ............................................... 5
3. Holiday Church Goer .................................... 10
4. True Love Does (NOT) Exist .......................... 15
5. The Gateway Drug ....................................... 21
6. All I Need in This Life of Sin Is Me and My
   Girlfriend ................................................... 29
7. Shackled by Lies .......................................... 34
8. It's All Fun and Games Until Your Best Friend Gets
   Murdered .................................................... 41
9. A Brilliantly Demonic Discovery .................... 45
10. High School and Hangovers ......................... 48
11. Chasing the Dragon .................................... 52
12. Get-Out-of-Jail Free Card ........................... 60
13. Selling Myself Short at a Breastaurant .......... 68
14. Things Back Home ..................................... 74
15. The Power of The Tongue ............................ 78
16. A Broken Hallelujah ................................... 86
17. New Start Ministry ..................................... 93
18. @Miriah_BornAgain .................................... 97
19. Hunger and Thirst for Righteousness ............ 104
20. Sleeping With the Street Preacher ................ 109
21. In the Waiting Season ................................ 118
22. "Handpicked" ............................................ 124
23. God Restored My Virginity .......................... 132
24. Memorial Stones ....................................... 138
25. Your Story Matters .................................... 142

Prompts to Help You Begin Sharing Your Story     147
My Prayer for You     149
Notes     151
Acknowledgments     153
About the Author     154

# FOREWORD

There are some books you simply read and then there are books that mark you. *The Unashamed Life* is one of those books.

Miriah Taverna's story is not just a recounting of her past. It is a living, breathing, fiery altar call to every heart who has ever believed that they were too far gone, too broken, too filthy for God to reach. This is not just a memoir—it is an invasion of the mercy and raw power of Jesus Christ.

I have had the sacred honor of walking with Miriah for years, watching the supernatural unfolding of her life firsthand. I have seen her rise from the ashes, not by willpower, not by religious striving, but by the relentless love of a Savior who simply refused to let her go. Every chapter of this book is soaked in that same relentless love, the kind that breaks chains, shatters lies, and calls the dead back to life.

Miriah's testimony is not pretty, but it is pure. It is not polished, but it is powerful. It is drenched in the kind of honesty and courage that few are willing to live, let alone write down for the world to see. She invites you into the deepest valleys of her life, not to glorify darkness, but to glorify the One who shines brightest in the darkest places.

Make no mistake. *The Unashamed Life* is an encounter, not just a book.

I believe that as you read Miriah's story, you will feel the grip of shame begin to break off your life. I believe the Holy Spirit will move through these pages to heal places you thought could never be healed. The same Jesus who met Miriah on a hospital bathroom floor, who pulled her out of demonic bondage and set her feet on solid ground, is ready to meet you too, right where you are.

This is not just Miriah's story. It is a prophetic call to a generation to rise up unashamed of the Gospel. It is a war cry to every believer who has been living with one foot in compromise and one foot in the Kingdom to come fully into the light. It is an invitation for the prodigals, the addicted, the abused, the abandoned —and even the "good churchgoers" who secretly feel like frauds —to step into true freedom.

The chains of yesterday will have no voice over those who dare to abandon all for true love. Christ's love. Shame is breaking. Graves are opening. The testimony of Jesus will roar like a mighty river through the lives of those who dare to believe that He is still the God who saves to the uttermost.

This is what *The Unashamed Life* carries—not just information, but impartation.

As you turn the pages, expect to be wrecked by His mercy. Expect to be gripped by conviction and overwhelmed by love. Expect to hear the Spirit of God whispering to you that your story matters, that your past is not too much for Him, and that your future is already written in His blood.

Miriah's life is a living memorial stone—proof that when the enemy says it's over, God says, "Watch what I will do."

She is a signpost to this generation that purity is possible, that deliverance is real, and that it is absolutely, gloriously worth it to follow Jesus with everything you have.

I am proud of Miriah beyond what words can express, not just because she survived hell, but because she chose to carry heaven into the very places the enemy thought he owned. She is not merely a survivor; she is a burning one, a forerunner, a voice crying out in the wilderness: "Prepare the way of the Lord. He is still the God who saves, delivers, heals, and restores."

As you read *The Unashamed Life,* know that you are not just reading someone else's story. You are being invited into a move of God that will shake your life, confront your past, and catapult you into the destiny He has prepared for you.

The same God who found Miriah in the pit, who delivered her from death, and who crowned her with glory, is reaching for you now.

You were never meant to live bound by shame.

You were never meant to hide behind your history.

You were born to live unashamed.

This is the hour. This is the call.

Step into the light and let the fire of His love consume you.

Tammie Southerland
Author of *Permission to Burn* and *Wordless Prayer*

# PREFACE

"Shame dies when stories are told in safe places."
- Ann Voskamp

In the pages of this book, you will read my story. The good, the bad, the ugly, and the *really* ugly. The unadulterated, raw, real-life testimony of how I was lost and now I'm found, of how I was dead and now I'm alive.

Every one of us has a story that needs to be told. Yours included. While you read through mine, I pray that God will show you how valuable your own story is and how He has been with you throughout every single step of your journey. When you know that God is The Author of your story, you can rest and experience joy throughout every chapter—even the really dark ones. I share my story without shame, in hopes that you, too, will be empowered to share your own story without shame.

## NOTE TO THE READER/TRIGGER WARNING:

Several names have been changed to protect the identity of others who were a part of my story.

In some parts of this book, I share my own struggles with grief, suicide, sex, and drug abuse.

# CHAPTER 1
# THE CHOICE IS YOURS

*… to whom much is given,*
*from him much will be required.*
Luke 12:48

Because of my continuous rebellion and disobedience while in school, my dad had been called to come in and meet with my fifth-grade teacher, Mr. West. We sat in blue plastic chairs around a half-moon-shaped table. My teacher didn't bash me. He didn't tear me down. He didn't say that I was a bad kid. Instead, he saw my potential, and he spoke to that place in me. He spoke to who God had created me to be.

"To those whom much is given, much is required," Mr. West said.

Those words gripped me. They're pretty much all I remembered from the parent-teacher conference that day. Mainly because my dad wouldn't let me forget them. He would continue to speak those words over me for years to come, even into my adult life. Even when I would make the worst of decisions.

In a way, Mr. West prophesied that truth over my future without me even knowing that it was *truth*. I didn't know at the time that this quote was actually a verse from Luke 12:48. I thought it was just a catchy quote that implied I was a leader. Ten-year-old Miriah didn't understand the *weight* of those words.

I also didn't understand that there was a God who made all the inner parts of me and thoughtfully knit me together in my mother's womb (See Psalm 139:13). Ten-year-old Miriah didn't know that God saw my unformed body and that every day of my life had been written in His book before I ever lived a single one. He had chosen me from before I was born. He had given me much, and therefore, much would be required of me.

I once heard someone say, "God has a plan for your life, and the devil has a plan for your life." I believe that God *does* have a plan for your life, and the devil has a plan to *destroy* your life. It's up to us which of those plans actually come to pass.

God created you with a plan. A purpose. A destiny.

God accepts you as *His own* because He alone created you— for *His* glory alone.

He created you for intimacy, that you might know Him. *He* made you. As the good Creator that He is, in all of His wisdom and creativity, He formed and fashioned you. He put His stamp of approval on you, and He called you *good*, long before the devil ever got the chance to call you bad. God called you *beautiful*, long before you ever got to look in the mirror and decide otherwise.

He created you for greatness, that He might put Himself on display in and through your life. With precious thoughts toward you as numerous as the sand on the seashore. His prosperous plans for you are beyond all you could ever dream.

I needed to know that at ten years old. I needed to know God's plan, but instead I fell into the trap of the devil and began, from a very young age, to believe his lies.

Going all the way back to the book of Genesis, we see that

God's original plan was never for us to endure hardship, tragedy, confusion, pain, loneliness, lostness, sin, or death. Yet, because we live in a fallen world, we experience darkness in ways that God never originally intended nor desired for us to experience. Some of which you will read about in the pages of this book. Despite the dark and difficult pages of my story, I believe that God is a good God, who has written a good story over my life. A redemptive story. And not only over my life, but over yours as well.

The beautiful thing is that in this one lifetime that we have to live, we get to make choices. Choice is a gift from God. We get to choose into witnessing God's plan for our life come to pass. Or not. The choice is entirely ours. Of course, there are many situations that arise in life that are beyond our control. Although we can't always choose what happens to us, we *can* choose how we respond.

Did you know that the average adult makes about 35,000 conscious choices per day?[1] In today's social media-drenched world, we are faced with a seemingly never-ending feed of choices. As I grew up, my dad used to always say this simple line to my siblings and I: "For every action, there is a reaction." My ten-year-old self could understand this concept. Action equals reaction, cause equals effect, choices equal consequences. But as I grew older, what I didn't fully comprehend was that every choice I made would either draw me closer to Jesus or pull me farther away from Him.

At some point along the way, every one of us will have to make the most important choice in life of all time. *Do you accept Jesus Christ as your Lord and Savior, or do you reject Him?* Everything else in your life hinges on this choice. It is *the* choice of all choices that you will ever make. And it is yours alone to make. No one can make it for you.

We cannot forget that after that initial choosing, we are presented afresh each day with a million little moments to choose Him again and again and again.

On the contrary, the devil wanted me to choose him. He wants all of us to choose him. Note that in choosing him, many of us don't outright say, "Yes, I choose to serve the devil." Not with those exact words, anyway. Instead, we subtly choose the devil when we choose to believe his lies. Once we choose to believe his lies, then our actions follow. And while we will never actually confess to serving the devil, the reality is that our actions speak loudly, and they are a language all of their own.

When we make the choice to believe the devil's lies, we ultimately begin to follow the devil's plan. At first, it may look enticing, feel innocent, and the consequences may seem nonexistent. But in the end, it leaves us empty, broken, and dead inside.

I know, because I did it. From a very young age, I began to believe the lie, *"No one loves me."* This would be the first lie of many that I would choose to put my faith in. And you are about to see how my own seemingly small choices began to reap big consequences in my life, as the devil pursued to destroy me.

# CHAPTER 2
# BORN INTO SIN

What if we allow the storms of life to be not just trials,
but teachers?

So, you know how I just said, "God has a plan for your life, and the devil has a plan to destroy your life?" Well, God's good plan is to give you peace, not evil, to give you a future and hope (See Jeremiah 29:11). But the devil's plan is to steal, to kill, and to destroy you (See John 10:10).

The devil understands that children are a gift from the Lord. He sees how children are like arrows in the hands of a warrior (See Psalm 127:4). He sees the purity, the innocence, the simple faith and love that children possess. Before a child even knows who God created him or her to be, the devil is already aware and is threatened by their existence. I think that is partly why he begins his pursuit to slaughter us and derail our destiny from the moment we are conceived in our mother's womb.

David writes in Psalm 51:5, "*Surely I was sinful at birth, sinful from the time my mother conceived me*" (NIV). This is true for all of us spiritually, but for me it was also true literally. I was conceived in sin, out of wedlock. My parents had been together for almost two years when Mama got pregnant with me.

Mama, a white woman, had gotten pregnant by Daddy, a black man. Even though slavery had been legally outlawed since 1863 when Abraham Lincoln signed the Emancipation Proclamation, and efforts to legally end segregation began in 1948 when President Harry Truman issued Executive Order 9981, racism was very much still alive in South Carolina in the early 1990s. In fact, very few people supported my parents' decision to be together as an interracial couple. Many were enraged when they found out that Mama was pregnant with a mixed baby, yet she chose life. She told me that even though she was scared to become a mom, she never once thought about aborting me. Mama carried me full term and birthed me into this world on Labor Day, September 6, 1993.

My parents loved each other the best that two people could. They desired to do what was right and to raise their new daughter to the best of their ability. Eleven days after I was born, my parents, along with my aunt as a witness, went down to the county courthouse and got married. Then they drove to Burger King and celebrated.

As children, sometimes we don't understand the depths of the things that our parents went through when they were children. We don't think to acknowledge them as human beings with thoughts, feelings, and emotions, dreams, desires, and needs. We see them only through the present lens of "Mom and Dad," often forgetting that "Mom and Dad" haven't always been a part of who they are and is *not* their sole identity. They are their own people with their own history, their own story, and a whole life that shaped them into who they are prior to ever becoming parents.

The devil is the author of despair and hopelessness, and childhood trauma left undealt with will often show up with a different face later on in our lives.

Depression is real. Postpartum depression is real. And unfortunately, it's the perfect breeding ground for the devil to sow lie after lie into a broken heart and vulnerable mind. Shortly after being home from the hospital, Mama found her mental state spiraling downward due to her own childhood trauma. Before she knew it, she was losing herself, slipping into a suicidal state, overcome with thoughts of harming not only herself, but me as well, her newborn baby girl. I believe that the devil's plan was to destroy us both. I'm forever thankful Mama chose to fight against those demonic attacks. That she chose to get herself the help that she needed so she could be the mom that I needed.

Overcoming the opinions of man—and to the enemy's demise—my parents chose love and life. Over and over and over again. Two years after they had me, my baby sister Sydney was born. And two years after that came my baby brother Holden.

I don't know all that was spoken of or thought of about me in the early days and early years of my life. But I have to believe that even in the midst of Satan pursuing to take my life that my heavenly Father, God, has always had His hand on me in a special way.

You see, the Holy Spirit of God is greater than any demonic spirit that could ever try to come against you. Despite the enemy's pursuit to destroy you from birth, or maybe even from your mother's womb, despite what's been done to you or said about you, you can overcome. You can rise up. God can turn your victimization into a victory, your test into a testimony, your mess into a message. And God can take everything that was meant to destroy you and work it for your good and for His glory (See Romans 8:28). He can bring beauty from your brokenness. He can turn your mourning into dancing and your tears into laughter (See Isaiah 61:3). He can redeem every single part of your life, if you allow Him. Ask me how I know.

It may not happen straight away. There are different types of storms, different categories, different intensities, even differences according to location and season. The storm may last for weeks, months, or even years, but no storm lasts forever. You may have to go through hell and high water before you see dry ground or a rainbow after the storm. Dancing in the rain is really fun … until the wind picks up and it's thundering and lightning all around you. Until you can't see where you're going, and you don't know if you're going to make it out.

I would say that my childhood was pretty bright and sunny. For the most part, stormless. Little did I know, the enemy rarely misses a chance to rain on someone's parade. But he doesn't always show up in a big, dramatic thunderstorm.

The devil is not dumb. He's been studying and interacting with humans for generations. He doesn't want us to walk in our God-given identity or to fulfill our God-given destiny. Behind the scenes, he cautiously and carefully sowed seeds (lies) into the rocky soil of my heart. These seeds took root beneath the surface, and he drizzled just enough rain in my life for them to sprout. Eventually, these seeds grew into trees that produced the most rotten of fruit. Trees that would weather the storms of life awaiting me ahead.

# CHAPTER 3
# HOLIDAY CHURCH GOER

*You believe that there is one God. Good!*
*Even the demons believe that—and shudder.*
James 2:19

Daddy was raised as a Jehovah's Witness. Mama was raised as a Pentecostal in the Church of God. And I was raised as a holiday church goer.

We went to Pentecostal churches on Easter, Mother's Day, Christmas, and random Sundays here and there. Sometimes, we'd even attend the Assembly at the Jehovah Witness Kingdom Hall. As we grew older, we played church basketball and went to church events, church plays, and church yard sales. Consistently inconsistent in our church attendance, we also hardly ever read the Bible at home.

I always loved it when we would go to church. I loved getting dressed up and feeling welcomed, loved, and accepted. Always knowing that we were going to have fun in children's church. The surety of there being fun arts and crafts projects and learning dance motions to a worship song. We'd get snacks, and then I'd get to play with my friends after service. I don't remember a lot of specifics about going to church in my childhood, but what I do have are joy-filled memories of people who loved God and seemed to love me too.

Looking back, I see Jesus throughout my story.

I know now that there were praying people all around me.

I even remember one specific thing my parents instilled in us as little kids. At bedtime, we always said these four words, "Don't forget to pray." Every night, my siblings and I would yell those four words from our bed down the hall to each other. "Don't forget to pray!" And while I have no idea what outrageous things I prayed for back then, I know without a shadow of a doubt that God heard my faith-filled, little girl prayers each and every time.

Never underestimate the power of simple, faith-filled prayers. It's never been about how eloquently we can word our prayers or how long and impressive they are. It's about our heart's focus with every word that we speak. It always has been. God is near to all who call on Him in truth, and His heart is turned toward the one whose heart is turned toward Him.

As I grew older and into middle school, I was able to make the decision for myself to begin attending a youth group, and I loved it. I went to Praise Cathedral Church of God most Wednesdays at 7PM throughout my sixth- and seventh-grade school years. Our youth group was called "The Net." I'll admit, my motives for going were way off and almost always involved some boy I liked, the free arcade games, and the café nachos I'd eat before service.

But deep down, in hindsight, worship always was my favorite part of it all. I always wanted to be up close enough to touch the stage. I wanted to be at the front of the altar, lifting my hands to heaven, even though I didn't fully understand that this posture signified full surrender to Jesus. Or maybe I did, deep in my heart of hearts.

I won't say that I got saved—born again—in middle school. I

honestly don't have a definitive moment as a child that I can look back on and say, "That's it! That's the day that I gave my life to Jesus!" But what I do have are definitive memories of praying "the sinner's prayer" every time a call to salvation was given at the end of a service. I would whisper those words over and over with my mouth. I really did believe in my heart that Jesus Christ died for my sins and that He rose from the dead.

The issue was, I wasn't living like I believed it. I resembled that wave of the sea the book of James talks about, blown and tossed by the wind, so double-minded and unstable in all of my ways. When you are half-hearted and wavering, it leaves you unstable. Can we really expect to receive anything from the Lord when we're in that condition?

And then it happened. In the midst of the storms, in the midst of me being tossed around at sea with no anchor for my young and confused soul, I slowly drifted away from church, which ultimately led me to drift farther and farther away from God.

I get it now, why it says in Hebrews 10:25, "… *not giving up meeting together.*" It matters, you know? Meeting together. Being around other believers. They stir us up in love and good works (See Hebrews 10:24). They keep us looking toward the One who really matters. They speak the truth into our souls, which washes us in love and hope, even when we're unaware of it. They pray for us and with us. There is something about true community that is a keeper.

Accountability? Yes. *But more than that.*

*Love.* Love keeps us. And when we neglect that love, when we neglect connecting with the believers around us, when we forsake it, it's a sure sign of a drifting heart … or a bitter one.

Eventually, I stopped going to youth group altogether, and even though I still called myself a Christian, the life that I began to live was anything but Christ-like.

As you drift from one thing, you can be certain that you're drifting toward something else. For me, that "something else" was the love, affection, and attention of others that I craved. I specifically wanted that love, affection, and attention from a guy. But I acted out in school in attempts to get it from teachers and my parents. I was so thirsty for it.

I didn't understand then the fullness of what was happening, but as I rejected and rebelled against God, I walked in rebellion in every other area of my life. I walked in this open resistance to any authority figure, anyone who tried to tell me what to do, and anyone who came against me in any way. I was constantly in and out of the principal's office, in ISS (in school suspension) and OSS (out of school suspension), in detention, getting referrals, and getting into fights. I was out of control.

Middle school is just a weird season of life for a lot of kids. With so many major transitions happening so fast, it can be challenging for many reasons, like puberty, peer pressure, and identity development. Throw on the added academic load and extra responsibility, and I was acting all the way up as I tried to navigate these big changes in conjunction with my big feelings and my big personality.

My parents and teachers tried to tarry with me. They tried to work with me. They saw the potential that I had. And they saw me throwing it all away. They would discipline me. Take my cell phone away. Ground me and take away my privileges. They had countless, hour-long talks with me about how my choices were not only affecting me, but everyone around me. They threatened to ship me off to boot camp or boarding school. My mom even wrote to Dr.Phil, asking to come on his TV show to see if he could help our family to get me under control. Which I honestly needed.

I was unruly in my defiance. My parents and teachers were at their wits end. My actions were overwhelmingly stressful to anyone that was connected to me. And I truly did not care. At this point in my life, I didn't care who I disrespected, who I let down, or who I hurt along the way. I honestly didn't understand the depth of the damage that I caused, but even if I would've known, I probably still wouldn't have cared.

All I cared about was what I wanted and how I wanted it and when I was going to get it. *Selfish* isn't a strong enough word to describe the utter egotistical attitude that I walked in every single day. And I was just getting started …

# CHAPTER 4
# TRUE LOVE DOES (NOT) EXIST

In every human heart lies the longing to love and be loved.
But is love alive? Or is love a lie?

At thirteen years young, I had no reason to venture through the wide gate and onto the broad road of destruction. I know now that it's not necessarily a set of circumstances that causes a person, young or old, to dive headfirst into a river of sin. But if it's not what's done to us that causes a person to make such choices, then what is it?

Simple. It's a lack of Truth in a person's life.

You can live the best life, go to the best schools, have the best jobs, the nicest cars, never struggle, and never really go through anything hard in your life, yet at the end of the day, you still end up choosing the river of sin and death over the river of Life and Truth.

Sure, our circumstances ultimately do play into why we do what we do and the choices that we make. But at the end of the day, it's simple. It's our lack of real relationship with Jesus. That is why we go astray. That's the root of it, anyway.

I didn't come from years of childhood trauma. I didn't come from a bad neighborhood or background. I didn't have a bad life. I wasn't horribly abused or neglected. I came from an average, middle-class family with a two-parent home. We played sports, drove nice cars, and had nice things. On the outside looking in, some would say we were the white-picket-fence type of family. Overall, I had a really great childhood.

*But that's precisely my point.*

Kids with great childhoods or kids with terrible childhoods. Either one can grow into a rebellious teenager, because rebellious teenagers don't come from a particular set of circumstances. Rebellious teenagers come from the lack of a personal relationship with Jesus Christ. They lack experiencing the love of God.

We all have a deep longing in us to be seen and loved and wanted. Every single one of us desire this from the time of our birth to the moment of our death. Deep down, even the hardest of hearts desire real connection, true intimacy, and genuine relationship, because it's what we were created for. God created us for real connection, true intimacy, and genuine relationship with Him and with others. We were created to be in communion with God and to walk with Him every day. His original design for us was utter bliss, perfection, purity, love, and freedom at all times. He made us in His image.

But why did God make us? Because He needed us? No.

He made us because He wanted us. He loves us. He made us for His pleasure because we are His delight. Because He wants us to experience the blessing of knowing and enjoying Him.

*But I didn't know any of that.*

You see, I had been exposed to pornography at a young age —seven. My secret dream, because I knew no better, was to grow up and become a porn star. I saw these beautiful women in these magazines. (Yes, if you were born after the 1990s, know that there was once a time when pornography was actually in magazines and on DVDs, long before it hit the World Wide Web.)

These women became my role models. Because what seven-year-old girl doesn't want to emulate a pretty woman with a nice body, wearing lots of makeup and sparkles and high heels? In my mind, I began to equate beauty with seduction, pornography with intimacy, and sex with love.

So, at thirteen years young, I wanted to be deeply loved. I wanted to be wanted. I wanted to be seen and heard. And because I had no clue Jesus already loved me deeply, wanted me, and saw and heard me, I went looking for that "love" in all the wrong places, in all the wrong people, and in all the wrong things.

My way of "loving" at thirteen years old became this: "If I love you, I will give you the most valuable part of myself." What was that most valuable part? My body, of course. The physical part of me. Oh, how wrong I was! Oh, if I had only known that the physical part of me is actually the least valuable part of me, for this body was made from dust, and one day it will return to dust (See Genesis 3:19).

The most valuable part of me is my heart, and that is what Jesus was after all along. But I didn't know that then.

The thing about young girls falling in love without first knowing Jesus' love is that it gets twisted up and misconstrued. Because my definition of love was far from Jesus' definition of love and was not rooted in Jesus' definition, that "love" destroyed my thirteen-year-old heart.

It all started with a guy named Jax. Shortly after we met and became friends, he asked me to be his girlfriend. It was my first "real relationship." I had played house with neighborhood kids and even had my first kiss years before Jax, but he was my first legit boyfriend. I truly loved him, to the extent that my young self could comprehend *love*.

Take a self-centered, rebellious, hormonal thirteen-year-old who doesn't know her worth and add into the mix a boyfriend who is also self-centered, rebellious, and hormonal. This is *not* a good recipe. Why didn't anyone tell my thirteen-year-old self that? I'm sure they did. But thirteen-year-olds know everything there is to know about life and can make their own decisions, right? I gave myself away. Laid down my innocence. Lost the one thing that we humans only have one of: my virginity. That was it. My virginity was there, and then it was gone.

I knew then as much as I know now that this wasn't the way that it was supposed to go. But it happened. I'd be with Jax forever now, right? He would love me forever now, right? I had given him my very best, so surely he would never leave now, right?

Two years later, he cheated on me with not one of my friends, but two different friends, two different times. My whole world flipped upside down. When your fifteen-year-old heart gets broken into a million pieces, it can break you all the way down.

After Jax and I officially ended things, devastation settled in. I entertained thoughts of taking my life, because I had made this boy my entire world. With him gone, it felt like my world was gone, like I had no reason left to live. If you have ever experienced a serious break up, then you know the feeling. That can't eat/can't sleep, close the blinds, shut off your phone, soak in R&B songs, and hide from the world feeling. That obsessive, *maybe things will still work out/I still want to be with the person who treated me like crap/I can't live without them* type of feeling. That *can't believe it's over/won't accept it's over/still holding on even though there's nothing to hold onto* kinda feeling. Yeah. That was me for years and years on end. Deep in my heart of hearts, I truly believed that Jax would come crawling back to me, and we would still live happily ever after.

I really think that we should stop telling young people they don't know what love is. Or that it's just puppy love. What young people really need from us is to be validated in their affections and emotions, no matter how shallow or superficial those affections and emotions may seem to us as adults. Breakups really do break hearts, and I don't think we can put an age limit on the degree of pain associated with each breakup or heartbreak. Heartbreak can lead to deep depression. And deep depression, in extreme cases can lead to suicide.

Did you know that in 2023, suicide was the second-leading cause of death among those between the ages of 15-24?[1] Nearly twenty percent of high school students report having serious thoughts of suicide, and nine percent have actually made an attempt to take their lives, according to the National Alliance on Mental Illness.

Even though I didn't actually attempt to commit suicide, I did contemplate it. I felt like I was dying inside. I couldn't live without this boy. Without him, it felt like life wasn't *worth* living anymore.

I'm just using this example to show you how important it is to validate teenage heartbreak.

We need to walk hand in hand with adolescents, so they don't lose themselves in the vulnerable space of heartbreak. It's important not to minimize their heartbreak, to see them where they're at, and point them to the Healer in the midst of their deep pain. To root them in the Love of God, so that when lesser lovers fail them, it doesn't kill them. It's extremely important that you give your children Jesus throughout their childhood. Before Christmas presents, birthday parties, and family vacations, He is what your children need the most. They need a foundation of how much Jesus loves them. They need Truth. But not just to be told truth. They need to be shown it. They need to see a truth-filled life lived out. They need to see the beauty of what it really looks like to know and experience God for themselves. The seeds that you sow will grow.

See, I didn't know Jesus' love. I didn't have someone teaching me about a relationship with the One who loves me enough that He gave His life for me.

As pain and loneliness consumed me, this heartbreak was

water and nourishment upon the deadly rooted seeds and lies that Satan had sown in my life years prior. Reiterating the lie that "no one loves me."

What I turned to next, at fifteen years old, would be the beginning of years and years of deep darkness, mostly because I needed to numb the pain of a broken heart.

# CHAPTER 5
# THE GATEWAY DRUG

Why is it so easy to go downhill, but so hard to climb up it?

Now a sophomore in high school, I wondered, *what am I doing with my life? Laying around and sulking in my misery?* I suddenly realized that I didn't have to wallow in this heartbreak. I didn't have to sit in this pain. While Jax and I were together, I'd dabbled in smoking cigarettes and weed here and there, recreationally, at parties. *I could numb this pain.* I could drink it away, smoke it away, party it away. And so, that's exactly what I began to do.

Smoking the occasional joint at a party turned into building personal relationships with drug dealers and getting my own drug stashes every week. I started to work a little part-time job at a local diner, and spent the money I earned on clothes, jewelry, alcohol, and weed.

Some say there are four types of gateway drugs: alcohol, marijuana, nicotine, and prescription drugs. I want to focus on weed for a minute. A lot of people today, especially with marijuana being legalized in many parts of America, will tell you that weed is absolutely, one hundred percent *not* a gateway drug. They will argue that it's a plant. They'll tell you it was "given to us by God." Or that they "can connect with God better when they're high." But one in ten people who smoke weed will become addicted to it.[1] Take it from someone who smoked weed all day, every day for years. It absolutely, one hundred percent *is* a gateway drug. Allow me to explain.

An article on *Web*MD describes how smoking weed can raise your chances of clinical depression or worsen the symptoms of any existing mental disorders that you already have. The article also touches on how smoking weed clouds your senses and judgment, ultimately distorting your thinking. Even more alarming is the fact that when young people smoke weed, it can interrupt their brain tissue development. That early exposure to smoking weed is also linked to changes in areas of the brain that are connected with psychosis.

Weed alters the way you function and removes your ability to respond the way that you would if you weren't under its influence. Just like alcohol or any other drug. Your level of impairment will differ depending on what and how much you take.

The reason I call weed "The Gateway Drug" is because, in many cases, it's the entry point into a whole world of other substances that dull your senses, alter your sobriety, and ultimately numb you to reality. I won't make the blanket statement that this is always the case, but in my personal experience, marijuana most definitely led to the use of more dangerous drugs.

I started with smoking weed and drinking alcohol all the time, and then I got introduced to pills and became hooked on Xanax and Adderall. After those, I added ecstasy/MDMA and then hallucinogens like mushrooms and acid/LSD. I was just a teenager having fun, right? I mean, I wasn't a drug addict, and I didn't have a drug problem *per se*.

I also swore I'd never be labeled a "coke head" or a "meth head." I mean, weed was okay, as long as I never did any of those more "hardcore" drugs, right? *Oh* so wrong! That spirit of addiction has its way of seducing you into itself without a care of what you become addicted to. As long as it's got you hooked, it's happy.

Why do we do that? Why do we categorize drugs into classes? Almost as if to say, "Weed addiction is okay. Pill addiction is okay. Sniffing a little recreational cocaine is okay. Trippin' on mushrooms or acid is okay. Rollin' on ecstasy is okay. But mention meth or heroin use, and all of a sudden, drugs are "bad for us." It makes zero sense to me.

And, just like we do with the sexual sin of homosexuality, we like to pinpoint certain drugs as if they are somehow worse than all the others. Why is it okay to be addicted to marijuana but not okay to be addicted to cocaine? Don't answer that. The point is this: addiction to *anything* will ruin you. Some addictions just ruin you faster than others.

One day, *it* happened. Someone presented me with an opportunity to try cocaine, and my previous promise to never do it slipped out of the window.

I thought, *Hmm, just one time won't hurt.* That mentality slowly began to ruin my life and my relationships. One time turned into two then into five then into fifty times. And "just a little bit more" turned into a whole lot more. Eventually, it turned into, "I'll do whatever it takes to get more." I don't even remember my first time snorting cocaine. All I remember was that I liked it and that I wanted more of it. A lot more of it.

Meth, on the other hand, now *that* was something that I absolutely, positively would never touch. To me, meth was trashy and cheap. And because it was unknown territory, I considered it a risk I was unwilling to take. I didn't even hang around "meth heads" or associate with anyone who smoked it, because to me that was one of those "next level" drugs, like fentanyl or heroin.

And so there I was, now sixteen years old and a functioning addict. Yet, I was in denial. My friends and I hung out with older people who would lend us their IDs and we would use those IDs to buy alcohol and sneak into nightclubs. We partied all the time. It was what we lived for. We had sex with whoever, whenever, wherever. It's purely God's grace that I'm still alive today to tell of it.

All the stupid things we did and places we went with complete strangers, who were completely obliterated. We drove drunk, slept around, and stayed high. We were out of control. And we loved every second of it. Consumed with sex, drugs, and money. I would frequently steal from my parents and from my little brother's money jar to scrounge up any dollar that I could. All to support my many out-of-control, unhealthy habits.

Basking in the dark dungeon of addiction, I sought to continually put myself into a drug psychosis where I would, in some weird way, be opened up to the spiritual realm. I believe that all drugs do this to some extent. Some more than others. You may meet people who say they "feel closer to God" when they're high. They may feel closer to something, to some god, but it's not the God that they think it is. Others say that they feel very far from God when they are high, and a lot of people even experience demonic encounters while on drugs.

That actually happened to me twice. These demonic encounters happened when I took psychedelics.

While with my friends one night, I decided to eat some mushrooms. I went outside of the apartment complex and looked around at the forest beside it, hoping to be inspired and to connect with the beauty of nature. But the opposite happened. The bark on the trees was not just regular tree bark. On every tree I saw an engraved, scary, demonic face. The branches danced and the bark wiggled, and the faces looked as if they were staring into my soul. Pierced with fear, I felt the darkness enclosing all around me, like it wanted to swallow me up. I remember being so uncomfortable looking at those trees that I ran back into the apartment and turned on all of the lights. I didn't want to be outside anymore. I didn't want to be in the dark anymore. I was able to switch my attention to happier thoughts once I was in the light. I stayed in the light and enjoyed the rest of my trip, but I never forgot that strange night. *Creepy.*

The other dark spiritual encounter that I had was on Halloween night (how 'bout that for a red flag). I took acid for the first and last time ever. I decided I wanted to take more acid than all of my friends. I walked up to this hippy-looking guy who had thick dreads that went past his waist and handed him my money. He pulled a glass vial from the inner pocket of his brown coat, then carefully squeezed the dropper twice into my mouth. I thought that it was taking too long to kick in, so I found a different dealer at the party to get a little bit more. He ripped off two small squares from what looked like a colorful sheet of cardstock paper and handed them to me. I chewed them up, rinsed them down, and waited. I had taken two liquid drops and two tabs. If you don't know anything about acid, just believe me when I say that is a decent amount of it. Especially being my first time ever taking it.

The hallucinations started about thirty minutes later, and that was fine. That's what I signed up for. I signed up for moving walls and twisting picture frames and sinking floors (think *Alice in Wonderland*). I signed up for strange sounds and heightened senses. But what I didn't sign up for was the spiritual part of this trip. It was just *way* too out of this world for me. It felt almost like I was in an alternate universe watching reality through a living kaleidoscope.

Colors looked more vibrant and vivid. Things that were small looked big. Things that were big looked small. Patterns on people's clothes danced, and people's faces melted if they were sad inside and radiated if they were happy.

I hadn't signed up to be able to look into people's eyes and see either light or darkness. I hadn't signed up to be able to intensely, physically feel the energy that other people operated in. This sounds crazy, but when I was on acid, it was like I could read people's inward heart motives without them saying a word. I could look at someone and see around them and on them and into them—in the realm of the spirit. I could feel their intentions and heart posture toward me in an unnatural yet physically tangible way.

In fact, what happened to me that night is hard to put into words. I remember how I felt, but I don't really have the vocabulary to explain it all.

Not only that, but this trip went on for a good sixteen hours straight. Nope, never again! Acid was a *no* for me.

There is something deeply spiritual about doing drugs, especially psychedelics. But just because something is spiritual doesn't mean that it's of God's Holy Spirit. Demons are spiritual too, you know?

My parents knew that I was out of control, but they didn't know how bad it actually was. Nor did they know how to help me. They did the best that they could—all they knew to do. Eventually, my mom ended up taking me to see a psychiatrist, thinking that he could help me.

It turned out that this particular doctor cared more about his paycheck and less about my issues and my hurting heart. Now, to his defense, I had zero intention of changing and every intention of taking full advantage of him. Getting him to write me a prescription for a controlled substance that I had pre-planned to turn around and abuse was all too easy.

Five minutes into my first "therapy" appointment, he literally asked me, "What do you need?"

I told him, "Something for anxiety."

A few questions later and *boom*, he wrote the prescription and out the door I went. It was like taking candy from a baby, except for this candy had the potential to destroy me, and this baby was all too eager to give it away. Now, I could legally numb my pain. *Klonopin*, also called *Clonazepam*, is a prescription pill that is used to treat panic disorders and anxiety. And now it was mine any time I wanted it.

Sadly, many doctors have sold out to pharmaceutical companies, which definitely influences their prescribing practices. Big pharma, a.k.a. the pharmaceutical industry, is a multi-billion-dollar industry. I am not anti-doctors or anti-modern medicine, because they do have their important and necessary place. There are some manufactured medicines that continue to save and increase the quality of life for many. But I am against doctors who are misusing their authority to prescribe highly addictive, modern medicines all for the sake of growing their own paycheck.

If you look at the fentanyl epidemic that our nation currently faces, it has been largely influenced and ushered in through the opioid epidemic which began in the mid 1990s.[2] In 1995, Purdue Pharma got Oxycontin approved by the FDA. Purdue Pharma then incentivized doctors to prescribe it in abundance, fully aware of how highly addictive it was, offering them payments for doing so. But that's a whole 'nother talk, for a whole 'nother day.

I don't remember who introduced me to the idea that it would be better to crush up those little yellow pills and snort them up my nose. As if swallowing triple and quadruple the number of pills that the doctor had recommended wasn't enough. But what I do remember is the slight burning in my nose as it went up my nostrils and how it instantly hit my brain. I remember the invigorating feeling, the adrenaline rush, and the high that seemed to desensitize me to everything around me and everything within me. Those little yellow pills gave me a supernatural ability to disconnect from the lie that I was unloved and the heartache that accompanied that lie.

I had become a master manipulator who cared about no one except for myself, all the while faking it for others and pretending that I didn't have any problems. I was truly a functioning addict. Some people will argue that there is no such thing as a functioning addict or a functioning alcoholic, but I beg to differ. What I mean when I use the phrase "functioning addict" is that I was able to somewhat maintain my jobs and relationships while being bound to consistent substance abuse. But one can only function as an addict for so long until it catches up with you. Malfunction is inevitable for the addict.

# CHAPTER 6
# ALL I NEED IN THIS LIFE OF SIN IS ME AND MY GIRLFRIEND

*"Love" apart from God is not love at all, but rather a distortion of what He intended it to be.*

O n top of the drugs, I was still looking for love in all the wrong places and still giving myself to all the wrong people. Then, things got even more twisted.

It hit me one day that "boys are stupid." Jax and every other guy I had chosen to give myself to were just *dumb*. Bitterness and unforgiveness took root in my broken heart, and that root had grown, causing me to resent all guys. So, I had the perfect solution for this resentment: Date girls instead! I started to identify as bisexual. All I really wanted was for someone to love me, and quite frankly, I didn't care if it was a guy or a girl who filled that position. I just wanted to love and be loved.

This goes back to what I said earlier about our hearts longing for attention. Longing to be seen, known, and loved. A lot of the time we don't really care where that attention comes from, as long as it comes. *And that's the problem.* The wrong attention from the wrong person with the wrong motives is just that—*wrong*.

We can never truly know true love until we know True Love. The One who sent His one and only Son into the world that we might live through Him (See John 3:16).

It's Jesus. *He* is Love. God loved us and sent His Son to die in our place. That's True Love. But when you don't know this Love, when you don't know this Jesus, there is no possible way for you to love another. Not purely, anyway. Not wholly. Not completely. Not selflessly.

So, how does a smart, athletic, gifted, talented, beautiful, and ambitious young lady even get to this place?

What started as a slow trickle quickly gained momentum. You could describe it like riding a bike down a hill. You don't have to exert much effort once you start rolling. The bike does most of the work for you. You simply sit there and enjoy the ride, letting it carry you from the top to the bottom. That's how it felt for me. Wind on my face, blowing my hair. On this bike, I felt free but didn't realize how bound I actually was. I was on a ride I thought I could get off of at any time. I thought I was in control of the bike, until I realized that it was in control of me.

Much of my teenage years are a blur because of all the drugs that I did. Addiction is a thief that seeks to kill, steal, and utterly destroy every person that it can. You think it will never be you, your child, your spouse, or your sibling, until it is. You see, addiction is no respecter of persons. It doesn't care who you are, where you're from, or what you stand for. It attempts to seduce everyone: the child and the elder, the male and the female, the doctor, the dentist, the teacher, the waitress, the single mom, the hard-working dad, the gold-medal athlete. Even the pastor, if not careful. The crazy thing is, when you're in the tunnel of addiction, you don't even realize how your world is rapidly disintegrating, or how time is wasting away, and life is passing you by.

It was the day after my seventeenth birthday when my parents kicked me out of their house.

Daddy pulled the "as long as you live under my roof, you live under my rules" line when he found out that I was in a serious relationship with a girl named Taylor. Although my parents were not super-devout Christians, they brought up the biblical story of Sodom and Gomorrah and reminded me of how God once destroyed an entire city for all of their sinful acts, one of those sins being homosexuality. Then, they told me that I had to make a choice. If I chose my relationship with Taylor, I could no longer live under their roof. If I chose living under their roof, I could no longer have a relationship with Taylor.

I do think it's interesting how we pinpoint homosexuality and single out this sin as if it's somehow worse than all the others. Why do we do that? Shouldn't we be against sin of every kind that keeps people from inheriting the kingdom of God? First Corinthians 6:9-10 encourages us to not be deceived or misled. It says that people who continue to engage in sexual immorality, idolatry, adultery, sexual perversion, fraud, greed, drunkenness, verbal abuse, extortion, or homosexuality will not inherit the kingdom of God. Did you notice how there are a lot more sins included in that list than just homosexuality? Not to mention the hidden sins of the heart, like lust, pride, and jealousy …

"It's Taylor or us" was the ultimatum my parents gave me. Who do you think I chose?

A few hours later, Taylor pulled into my parents' driveway on Belgray Court to pick me up. I gathered as much of my stuff that we could fit into her little, black '98 Honda Accord, and as it rained, we drove away to begin our new life together. I was a little scared but mostly excited. The adrenaline pumping through my body felt good, like another drug that I could enjoy in my most current rebellious adventure.

I can only imagine now how my parents must have felt watching us drive off through their tear-blurred eyes and under foggy skies. They watched their first baby girl slip through the cracks and disappear from their sight out into the big, bad world. I think they knew that the world was gonna chew me up and spit me out. And deep down, they knew that was exactly what I needed: to be chewed up and spit out. They were so brave to let me go, even though they didn't really have a choice.

I remember feeling so angry at my parents for their judgment toward me. Feeling like they handled the whole situation wrong. Feeling like an entitled victim. I didn't want to own any of my wrong actions toward them for the past four years. I only wanted them to own their wrong actions toward me regarding my relationship with Taylor.

Them kicking me out felt like I was being both rejected and released all at the same time. Rejected, because their decision solidified the lie that I was unloved and unwanted all the more. Released, because I thought that I would be independent and free. I thought I knew what it took to live on my own, and I thought that no parents meant no rules, no curfews, no punishments, and no accountability. I was in for a rude awakening.

But I was okay with it as long as I was able to love and be loved. And that is what I thought I had found in Taylor. Someone to love me, as deep and wide as the day is long.

There's a verse in the Bible that says, *"Above all, love each other deeply, because love covers over a multitude of sins"* (1 Peter 4:8). I find it super interesting that when I was in my lowest moments, the people I was willing to listen to the most were the ones who showed me the most love. Let's not get it twisted; love is not the same as acceptance. But love really *does* look like something.

I'm sure you've heard it said, "Love the sinner. Hate the sin." There is a way to speak the truth in love. Lisa Bevere once wrote, "Truth without love is mean, but love without truth is meaningless."[1] Deep down, I wanted to know the truth. But first I needed to know that I was loved.

Personally, I believe that love dismantles walls. There's something about pure, unconditional love that can break through even the hardest exterior, because at the core of every human being, we're created to love and be loved.

They say the only thing harder than being an addict is loving one. I remember my younger sister, Sydney, loving me so well when I moved out and moved in with Taylor. She wasn't even trying to love me in a way that made me feel that loved, and I guess that's what makes it even more beautiful. Her authentic, pure love when I felt like I was an unlovable, gay, strung-out addict, kept me. Her phone calls just to see how I was doing—and probably to make sure I was still alive—kept me. Knowing that she cared, even though my actions were destroying our family, kept me.

When you're in that swirl of active addiction, days turn into weeks, and weeks turn into months. You miss birthday parties and holidays. You burn bridges with those you love the most. You not only destroy relationships, but drug addiction alone is self-harm in so many ways with the havoc that it wreaks on your entire body. Talking to Sydney was sobering for a moment, but as soon as we hung up the phone, I was right back to having to deal with myself—my own worst enemy. Right back to needing to numb the pain and escape reality. And right back to running from myself and, ultimately, running from God.

Circling back to that bike illustration and pondering how I even got to this place …

It literally all happened so fast. With one selfish decision after another, I rolled faster and farther downhill. It seemed like a never-ending ride down a never-ending hill. Rock bottom was somewhere way down there, but I hadn't hit it yet. All gas and no brakes seems like fun, until it's time to slow down and you're unable to stop.

In hindsight, I didn't even realize how far down the hill I had fallen until I looked up and had no idea where I was or who I was anymore.

# CHAPTER 7
# SHACKLED BY LIES

What is freedom of the body when the soul is still in chains?

The first couple of weeks living with Taylor were great, and then reality set in. This new reality meant that I was now in charge of my own life in a different way. I was a junior in high school, and this new freedom meant that it was *my own* responsibility to get up and get to school on time. *My own* responsibility to buy groceries and feed myself. *My own* responsibility to pay my phone bill and my portion of the rent. All things I didn't have to even think twice about when I was living at my parents' house. Which meant I needed to pick up extra shifts at my waitressing job. And that my part-time paycheck, which used to be play money to spend however my little heart desired, was now a necessity for me to survive.

So here I am, a functioning addict, living with my girlfriend, struggling in school, and consumed by my own desires. Taylor and I were doing what we needed to do in order to make it through each day and support our extremely expensive daily habits of smoking cigarettes and weed, popping pills, and snorting cocaine.

Months and months of going through the motions ensued. Drugs, parties, sex, more drugs, more parties, more sex. It got to the point where Taylor and I even began inviting other people into the bedroom with us. It's shameful to mention the things that we did behind closed doors.

This way of life had become every day, normal life to me.

While I still occasionally showed up for school, I asked myself, *What's the point?* I was failing all my classes. I rarely went to school, and when I was there, I wasn't in my right mind, or I would leave early. I was living way below my means—my intellectual means. I was barely making it through the eleventh grade, while I'd scraped by pretty good in ninth and tenth grade. My high school career had begun with great attendance, decent grades, and running on the track team. I was the same girl who had placed in spelling bees, won "Terrific Kid," writing, and reading awards, was in gifted and talented challenge classes, and remained on the A/B honor roll all through elementary school. How had I let myself fall this far?

One day, I finally had enough of going through the motions. I met with the guidance counselor and told her that I'd decided to drop out of school. I'd told her I was eventually going to get my GED, but honestly I had no real plans of ever doing so. And just like that, I signed some papers and was out the door.

I never imagined myself dropping out of high school. And I'll be honest. Even through all the drugs that numbed my emotions, I had this slight disappointment in myself for dropping out that I could feel deep in the pit of my belly. But I pushed past that feeling and pushed forward to freedom. Or to what I thought would be freedom, anyway. Little did I know that this "freedom" I was running after would lead me straight into a literal jail cell. I'd soon be locked up in GCDC, Greenville County Detention Center.

We'd gotten pulled over while driving down Wade Hampton

Boulevard for throwing a cigarette butt out of the car window. Apparently, you're not supposed to do that. The officer walked up to the driver's side door, and right away he smelled the scent of weed lingering in the car from when we'd smoked it about an hour earlier. He had us get out and called for backup.

The cop offered for us to sit in the back of his cop car so we could keep warm while he, the other officers, and the K9 dog searched our car. He was a kind officer—many of them are—but when you're a law breaker, you want nothing to do with the police, even the kindest of them. I still remember how we trembled from the freezing temperature that night. We took him up on his offer and sat waiting in the back of his cop car, warm, anxious, and uncuffed, locked in on both sides with a thick glass separating the back seat from the front.

Almost instantly, he found a baggie of pills underneath the driver's seat. I had no clue what kind of pills they were or where they'd come from, and I didn't really think anything of them at first. They continued their search and also found our weed pipes, grinders, and weighing scales.

While we waited, Taylor whispered, "Tell the cop that the bag of pills is yours."

"Huh?" I whispered back, even though I'd heard what she'd said loud and clear. I was quickly mentally processing that statement, shocked that she would ask that of me ... but not really. "No, I don't want to go to jail," I muttered after a few seconds.

"You will only be in there overnight. You're a minor, so they can't hold you long. First thing in the morning, you'll be able to sign yourself out," she said.

Scared to my core, I put on my big girl panties and thought to myself, *Okay. I'm a ride-or-die chick, surely I can do one night in jail.*

As the officer typed away on his car's laptop, looking up each of the pills that were in that baggie, he told us, "If these are Advil or some over-the-counter medicines, I'll write you guys a ticket for the drug paraphernalia, and you'll be free to go. But if they're not over-the-counter medicines, then someone is going to jail tonight."

Time stood still for me as he typed a description of each pill into his computer system and waited patiently on the results. I don't remember how much time passed before he asked us to get out of the car. Maybe twenty minutes? Maybe thirty? But I do remember when he told us that the pills in the baggie were Schedule 2 and Schedule 4 narcotics. They most definitely weren't over-the-counter meds.

We got out of his car, and as we stood freezing on the side of a busy road, he asked us a series of questions.

After a few minutes, I spoke up. "Officer, those pills are mine."

He looked confused, as if he knew that I was lying. "Are you sure?"

I insisted that I was sure, and eventually he cuffed me and drove me downtown to book me. I concocted a whole story and timeline of how I'd gotten the pills from a guy I knew. I signed some paperwork, gave him my fingerprints, and then he led me to the showers, where they took my cute, comfy clothes and handed me an oversized, bright-orange jumpsuit in exchange. After I changed, they cuffed my hands and ankles and led me to take my mugshot. Then, they chain-linked me to the other women who were being booked in and put us all in a holding cell before transporting us down to our personal cells.

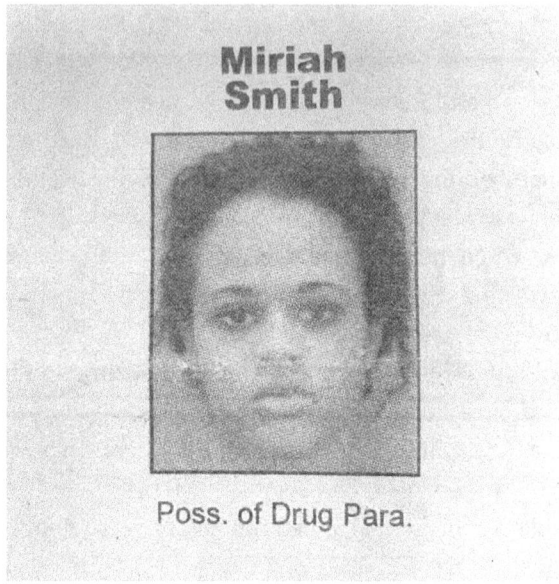

Miriah
Smith

Poss. of Drug Para.

My pod felt so cold and bare and stale. Bright-white lights overhead reflected off of the brick walls, and even though everything was fully lit, it was so dark in there. The colorlessness made it feel all the more lifeless and hopeless. All of the pods were hollow and empty except for a little metal cot, a little metal sink, and a little metal toilet. There wasn't even a mirror in there. There was one very small, barred window that I could peek out of to see part of the highway and a few leafless trees in the dead of winter.

I felt so out of place. I was ready to hurry up and go to sleep so that I could wake up and get out of this place. I was hungry. I was scared. My hair was a mess. I felt gross and dirty. *I don't belong here,* I thought to myself. *I'm seventeen years old. A juvenile.*

The sun rose the next morning, and I just knew I was leaving to go home. But when I asked the correction officer on duty when I would be able to sign myself out, she told me, "Honey, they booked you in as an adult. You're not getting out of here until someone posts your bond." Apparently, in the state of

South Carolina, people seventeen years old and older *can* be charged as adults for crimes. *Hmm, who knew?*

When the hour came that we were able to use the phones, I called Taylor, and she swore that she would bail me out. I waited and waited for her to come through, ringing her phone endlessly for two days before I finally realized that she wasn't coming. And I knew that if I wanted anyone to pay my bond, I was going to have to work up the courage to make a phone call that I *really* didn't want to make. I was going to have to call my parents.

As I write this book years later, a lot of the memories from my past seem like a distant blur to me. But I remember the day that I called my daddy from the county jail very, *very* clearly. After we talked for a while, he agreed to bail me out on three conditions: One, I move back home. Two, I break up with Taylor. Three, I go back to high school.

I agreed. "Yes, yes, and yes, just get me out of here."

If you've ever known a drug addict, you know that they are master manipulators and will say or do just about anything to get their way. I would've said anything to get out of that place.

A horrible winter snowstorm delayed my escape for a whole seven days. But my parents paid my bond, and after a week had passed, I was finally able to stand before the jail judge and be released.

Daddy picked me up, and I spent one full night at home before I called Taylor to come and get me. I only cared about what I wanted, and it didn't matter to me whose heart I hurt along the way. I had slapped my parents in the face yet again.

How in the world could I do such a thing?

True insanity. I went right back to what I knew and what I wanted. Back to the same girl that had just used me and left me in jail for dead. Something in me still wanted to be in this relationship. I thought surely our relationship would be stronger now that I had taken these charges for her. But it turns out things were quite the opposite, especially after I found out that she had been cheating on me with her ex—who had given her that incriminating baggie of pills—the whole week that I was locked up.

It took about four more toxic months of being reunited and moving back in with Taylor before we came to see, on our own terms, that this relationship wasn't healthy for either of us and it just wasn't going to work out. To her defense, today, fourteen years later, she has changed so much. And I wasn't the world's best girlfriend either. I was just as toxic, just as selfish, and just as out of my mind as she was. We were like fire and gasoline. Taylor and I ended our relationship. All those charges, all that jail time, all those burned bridges. All that, *for nothing*!

Where was I to go, and what was I to do now?

The nerve that I had to call my parents, yet again, and ask to move back home after the stunt that I just pulled was ballsy. Yet, they welcomed me back with open arms. Sounds like another story you may have heard before. Their prodigal daughter had returned home, again. Except, unlike the son in the biblical story of Luke chapter fifteen, I hadn't actually "come to my senses" just yet. I wasn't ready to humble myself and confess that I had sinned against heaven and against my parents. I was still very much lost.

I moved back into my parents' house, for real this time, and it felt like I'd taken 100 steps backward. I continued in the fakery of wearing the "I've changed my ways" mask. But beneath that mask was the same ol' girl, with the same ol' hard heart, the same selfish desires, and the same controlling addictions.

# CHAPTER 8

# IT'S ALL FUN AND GAMES UNTIL YOUR BEST FRIEND GETS MURDERED

Death and losing someone that you love has its way of shaking us. Sometimes it shakes us into being better, but sometimes not.

I can still see Amber's smile and hear her laugh as I write this, thirteen years later. She had a laugh like no other. She was my first middle-school friend and the one always willing to dance and rap with me. We knew every single word to Lil Wayne's "Get Em." To me, Amber was a lily blowing in the wind and a shot of Everclear, with no chaser. She was a soft, gentle hug alongside a hard, rapid punch. A lover when she loved and a fighter when she fought. She was a friend that I could trust, whether we'd stolen a canned squirt cheese and eaten it in the grocery store or made a fake social media page to stalk people and stir up teenaged drama. She was my El Jalisco, chips, and queso partner.

She's the only friend I've ever fist fought with and then made up within the hour. She was the one I could talk with for hours about my hidden drug addiction and not once did she judge me. Because she had her own. Except hers was not so hidden. In a way, I admired her, because she didn't have to live a double life like I did. The heartbreaking thing is that she barely got to live a life at all.

I still remember when I got the phone call that something had happened to Amber. It was April 3rd, 2011. Two nights prior, Taylor, Amber, some friends, and I were all hanging out drinking and smoking like we did every night. (Taylor and I continued to party together, even though we were no longer dating.) During this particular season of her life, meth was Amber's drug of choice.

Meth, in my opinion, is probably the worst drug out there, next to fentanyl. I have another name for meth. I literally call that drug "the devil." Meth makes you delirious. It makes you so out of your mind that you will do the craziest things, all while believing that what you're doing isn't crazy at all. It can cause you to be extremely paranoid, to hallucinate, to pick at your face for hours, causing "meth sores." It can cause memory loss, breathing problems, sleep deprivation, and aggressive, violent behavior. Some synonyms for violent are *brutal, vicious, homicidal,* and *murderous.*

And that is exactly what three guys who were on meth did to my best friend. They were brutal, vicious, and homicidal. *They murdered her.*

They brutally beat her, and as if that wasn't enough, they then shot her six times.

They also shot Chris, the guy that she was with, twice.

Then they set the house on fire and left their bodies to burn before the fire department came to extinguish it and to discover the gruesome crime scene of a double homicide.

When I heard that Amber had been murdered, I was shaken, shocked, and heartbroken. I still miss her like crazy and occasionally visit her grave. Sometimes I wonder what life would be like if she was still here. I wonder if she might have come to know Jesus too. If she might have experienced the freedom He brings and the depths of His love. If we might still be best friends. My guess is we would.

It took four full years before those three guys were locked away in prison in 2015, and I thank God for that little glimmer of justice. But justice didn't bring back my best friend.

Amber was only eighteen years old when her life was taken from her. Though, truth be told, drugs begin to take your life long before you ever take your last breath. Drugs take your peace, your joy, your relationships, your motivation, your dreams, your desires. They take it all and give you counterfeit peace and joy and counterfeit, temporary relationships. Your motivation, dreams, and ambitious desires slowly fade away. In their place, you're given this illusion that makes it seem like you're living life, but in reality you're dying a slow death while breaking the hearts of the people who truly love you along the way.

You would think that losing my eighteen-year-old best friend in such a tragic way would have woken me up to the reality of how short life really is. That it would have helped me get my act together and stop doing drugs. That it would be through losing her that I would hit rock bottom and give my life over to Jesus.

But instead, I did the complete opposite.

I followed head-first into Amber's footsteps. My coined slogan for this season of my life was inspired by Drake's song, "The Motto." My motto became, "YOLO! You Only Live Once."

And that is true. Each of us will only live once and only die once. Even Hebrews 9:27 says, "*It is in the plan that all men die once. After that, they will stand before God and be judged*" (NLV). But the thing about me was that I wasn't YOLOing for God. I was living for myself and for the devil. I thought, *If YOLO is true, and you only live once, then I might as well have as much fun as I can, indulging in all that the world has to offer, and living every day like it's my last.*

And that's exactly what I set out to do.

# CHAPTER 9
# A BRILLIANTLY DEMONIC DISCOVERY

Before 2011, I would say that I had my addiction under control.
But now I know you can never have an addiction under control.
It always has you under its control.

My addiction had gotten to the point where I had to have cocaine almost daily, and on the days that I didn't have any, I busied myself with plotting on how I was going to get some. You know that drugs have become a major problem in your life when what was once only recreational use turns into mostly personal use. I became greedy. I wanted the cocaine all to myself. I would pick it up by myself, and I would keep it to myself. It was no longer appealing to me to do a little bump here or there with my friends. I had become dependent on it in such a way that I didn't want anyone to know when I had some on me, because if they knew I had it, that meant that I'd have to share it. Cocaine was too expensive to be shared. Social, casual cocaine use was a thing of the past; it was now a habitual necessity.

I made the brilliantly demonic discovery that I could sell my body for lots of drugs and lots of money in the summer of 2011. My cocaine addiction was at an all-time high, and it was getting harder and harder to sustain because my little part-time income didn't supply enough to support my full-time addiction. I had done sexual favors in exchange for smaller amounts of drugs a couple of times before, but those oral favors no longer compensated for the amount of cocaine that my body cried out for. I was going to have to up the ante. When I decided to take it to the next level, my cocaine payment for these favors tripled and included a little cash too.

I had no clue that I was supposed to honor and glorify God with my body. No clue that I was His most expensive purchase, bought at the highest price by His precious blood. I didn't understand what the precious blood of Jesus really even meant. That the Bible teaches that without the shedding of blood, there is no forgiveness of sins. I didn't know that when Jesus was shedding His blood on the cross, He was thinking of me. I had no clue that He wanted me that badly. That He loved me so intensely. That He had paid a price for me that my drug dealers never could.

Having an addiction of any kind isn't cheap. Some people's minds are blown when they realize how much money the average addict spends on their addiction. Almost everyone is familiar, to some extent, with addictions that involve the use of substances, such as drugs or alcohol. Yet, little attention is given to other addictions like pornography, cell phones, social media, video games, food, coffee, gambling, or sex. My mind was blown when I realized how ready and willing people were to pay for sex. Broken sex addicts fuel a large demand, and broken people provide the large supply.

I dove in headfirst to take advantage of their desperation so that I could make ends meet in my own desperation. I surrendered myself to one cocaine dealer after another after another in exchange for a little baggie of white powder and a piece of paper with Benjamin Franklin on the front. In order to do what was necessary to score, I had to be heavily intoxicated, always under the influence of some substance. Often I drank alcohol or took Xanax or both.

I always felt disgusted with myself and the entire situation while participating, counting down the seconds until they were relieved. In real time, it hardly ever lasted long. But to me, ten minutes felt like an eternity.

Afterward came the most uneasy part. Deep down, I dreaded the eye contact that came at the end of each encounter, when I was to receive my payment. Yet, I did it anyway. I was a full-blown drug fiend, and my addiction was stronger than my dignity. Everything in me craved cocaine more than my next breath, and I was willing to do whatever outrageous thing I had to in order to keep a baggie full of it in my wallet at all times.

One thing about stimulant drugs—or as we used to call them, *uppers*—is that they suppress your appetite and increase your metabolism. Because I spent so much of my time getting and doing cocaine, I spent less time eating food and less money buying food. I lost so much weight I was just skin and bones, my cheeks were hollow, and my eyes dark and lifeless. I looked sick, because I was sick. I was terribly sick with a disease called *drug addiction*. I didn't know that I was in need of a doctor and some type of treatment. The thing about spiraling out of control is that you hardly realize it until you've already spiraled out.

What has always been amazing to me is that throughout my story, even in the midst of my darkest moments, I can still look back and see the Lord's hand all over my life. I can see how He kept me when I didn't even want to be kept. How He protected me when I didn't even know I needed protecting. And how He was always watching over me, even when I thought that no one saw my hidden deeds. He saw me go into every crack house, do every drug deal, tell every lie, steal every penny, sleep with every stranger … He saw it all. And instead of letting me die in my sin, He had mercy on me. So much mercy on me.

But I had yet to discover this truth.

# CHAPTER 10
# HIGH SCHOOL AND HANGOVERS

With eyes wide, dilated, and dark I continued going through
the motions, hoping to conceal my addictions that were
hidden in plain sight.

When August rolled around, I re-enrolled at
Eastside High School. With all gas and no brakes, I
put on my big girl panties, crushed and snorted
some pills, and began the 2011-2012 school year.

When they handed me my school ID and lanyard, I hung it
around my neck with shame. Since I'd made the brilliant decision to drop out during the middle of my junior year, big, black
numbers announced that I remained in eleventh grade. The
school placed me in an eleventh-grade homeroom and gave me
classes with all juniors. Talk about embarrassing.

I had a full schedule of eleven classes. Seven day classes, two
night classes, and two online classes. All of my school friends
were in their senior year of high school, which meant that most
of them had a half day of classes and left school around
lunchtime. But not me. I'd determined to walk across that stage

and graduate with my original class of 2012. The guidance coun-selor told me it was possible, but it would take a lot of work on my end.

"I can do it," I told her. I remember thinking, *even though I'm highly addicted to cocaine, I can do it. I can finish school, and I can graduate with my class.* The motivation to graduate was one percent to please my parents and ninety-nine percent rooted in the fact that I wanted to experience high school life for just a little bit longer—you know, all the pep rallies and football games, the parties, and prom. The extravert in me loves that kind of stuff. Oh yeah, did I mention the parties?

It was wild how I could compartmentalize certain parts of my life. When at school, I focused on graduating. When I wasn't at school, I focused on getting high. It was like a light switch that I could flip on and off. Weekdays were for school stuff, a little cocaine, and lots and lots of cigarettes. Thursday, Friday, and Saturday were for clubs and parties and lots and lots of alcohol.

In this season, I became more addicted to alcohol than I'd

ever been before. With my fake ID, I could buy a bottle of wine or a canned, hard cider or tea any time I wanted. Which means I always had alcohol, because there's never a time when someone in active addiction isn't in want.

We don't always see alcoholism in the same light that we see drug addiction. Maybe because drinking alcohol is legal, and therefore it's normalized in most recreational settings. But there are tons of negative consequences associated with alcohol misuse. Alcohol plays a factor in about twenty-five percent of suicides, fifty percent of homicides, fifty percent of fatal drownings, and thirty-one percent of car crash fatalities.[1] We really shouldn't downplay alcoholism at all, seeing that alcohol-related deaths continue to increase in America.

Alcohol affects your physical and emotional health too. For me, it greatly numbed my pain, making it yet another tool in my arsenal of substances that helped me escape reality.

While alcohol was the cherry on top of my drug sundae, I couldn't go to school drunk.

Wednesdays and Thursdays were my favorite days—the two days that I had to snort coke. As long as I gave myself those seventy-two hours to detox for my weekly drug test, I was good. I had this hot-pink, brand-name wallet with a gold zipper on it. That wallet had a bunch of different compartments in it, and I always kept a small baggie filled with powder tucked into the corner of one of those compartments. I stopped into the school bathrooms between classes or during a break and took little bumps of cocaine to get me through the day. I also frequented the stairwell on the back side of the school—near Mrs. Waller's French class—throughout the day for cigarette breaks.

I'm not sure how I didn't lose the motivation for school in the midst of everything, but it was as if the thrill of it all kept me going. Anything that could get me high enough, distracted enough, or busy enough to escape reality was a go in my book. The excitement of my "hidden" drug addiction felt like I was living a double life at times. And that was its own type of high in and of itself.

# CHAPTER 11
## CHASING THE DRAGON

Little by little, I slipped away, until I stood before the mirror
and saw a stranger staring back.

Remember that bicycle analogy I talked about back in
chapter six? At this point, I'm still on that ride, and
believe it or not, I'd just begun to really pick up the
speed. Things began to get bad. Really, really bad. One foot in
front of the other, I continued in this deceptive revelry. And I
followed in my dear friend Amber's footsteps, headfirst, down a
path I swore I would never go.

Since I had tasted the freedoms of being outside of those four
brick walls, my brain still craved those freedoms. Yet, I was back
in this prison called high school. Maybe if I stayed busy enough,
that would prevent me from breaking out again. I hung out with
everyone: whites, blacks, Hispanics, popular kids, non-popular
kids. It made no difference to me. I just wanted a good time and
to be the center of attention at that good time. And if I couldn't
find a good time, I created one.

We started our days in homeroom. This classroom was also

where we would go on days of state-wide testing and different things like that. In my homeroom with Mrs. Hughey, which was full of juniors, I made a friend.

Her name was Carissa. You know how you meet certain people, and you instantly click with them? That's what happened with me and Carissa. Honestly, that's what happened with me and a lot of people. I know now that kindred spirits attract one another. The wild party girl in me recognized the wild party girl in her. Or you could say, the spirit of addiction in me recognized the spirit of addiction in her. Truth be told, it was more than that though. Carissa was a genuinely down-to-earth, kind, funny, outgoing, lovely girl.

We quickly became besties, and we were inseparable. Without much effort at all, we started to do life together. We hung out all the time. I introduced her to my friends, and she introduced me to hers. And after just a few months of friendship, I introduced sweet Carissa to my lifestyle of cocaine addiction and showed her how I used my body to get what I wanted. On December 16, 2011, we were chillin' at one of her friends' houses when sweet Carissa wanted to introduce *me* to something.

Used to smoking weed out of colorful, glass-blown pieces, this was the first time I had ever seen someone smoke out of a clear, wand-looking bowl. Curious as I was, I watched them pour a little baggie of what looked like frosted, tiny pieces of glass shards into this clear pipe. As they held a lighter over the bottom of the shards, smoke filled the bubble at the end of the pipe, and they slowly inhaled whatever that stuff was that was in it.

At first, I thought, *is it crack?* I've smoked cocaine before, and that was similar to crack. But this stuff was slightly different. The consistency and color of it was different.

I sat there, taking it all in, kind of scared but kind of intrigued. The guy holding the pipe passed it to the other people in the room, and I watched them all inhale it like they were drinking in something sweet and smooth. They made it look really appetizing.

Then someone asked me, "Wanna hit it?"

Everything in my gut screamed, "Don't do it. This isn't right." And for a millisecond I thought, *what if it kills me? What if I become strung out on it? What if it's laced with something?* All those thoughts came and quickly went before I blurted out my excuse, "I can't. I get drug tested every week."

Then someone said, "But it'll only stay in your system for seventy-two hours."

*Ding, ding, ding.* Those were the magic words that I *didn't* need to hear.

"Okay then. I've never done this before, but sure, I'll hit it one time." I didn't need to vocalize the question I wrestled with internally. Deep down in my heart of hearts, I knew exactly what those little glass shards were.

They lit up the bottom part of the pipe with a small blow torch, it filled up with smoke, and they gave me my cue. "Inhale now."

Instantaneously, I ascended into a high that blew my mind.

A distant memory now, I can't tell you my exact thoughts that followed in the moments after I smoked crystal meth for the first time. But I can tell you that I enjoyed it. It was unlike any other high I had experienced in my life. The best word that I can use to describe it is *euphoric.* I won't call it heavenly, but it was most definitely other worldly. It was a type of out-of-body experience. But more like out of mind. It seemed to have opened up a part of my brain that I had never accessed before. I wasn't hallucinating, but I was. It wasn't hallucination in the same way that shrooms or acid cause one to hallucinate. It was more of a mental hallucination, like I could feel the chemistry in my mind and body shifting. This sudden rush of pleasure and prolonged sense of euphoria, combined with the crazy energy that it gave me, felt almost like I had a superpower. All I knew was that I liked this feeling. And that I wanted more.

I know now why meth is so highly addictive. It's because meth releases a surge of dopamine in the body. Dopamine is a type of hormone and neurotransmitter made in our brains that is associated with feelings of pleasure or reward. As a neurotransmitter, it affects things like our movement, memory, motivation, and mood. As a hormone, dopamine is released into our bloodstream and plays a role in our fight-or-flight syndrome. In other words, dopamine could be called the feel-good hormone. It gives us our sense of pleasure, as well as the motivation to do things when we feel that pleasure. Dopamine is a part of our brain's reward system, and a large amount of it gets released into our body whenever we do something pleasurable. When we feel good, we seek out more of that good feeling. Dopamine is also why things like junk food, sugar, sex, exercise, or shopping can be so addictive. They make us feel happy, and we want to repeat those happy experiences again and again.

But the dark side to dopamine is that people get this same "happiness" when they take drugs, such as cocaine, heroin, or in this case, meth. All drug abuse causes the release of dopamine—even alcohol and nicotine. But, it has been said that methamphetamine produces the mother of all dopamine releases.[1]

Have you ever heard the phrase "Chasing the Dragon?" It's a phrase used in the drug world that refers to smoking a controlled substance, often heroin. But the root meaning of "chasing the dragon" is desperately chasing an unattainable feeling. Chasing something that you'll never catch.

For the next five months, I chased the dragon. I tried to catch the high that I encountered that very first time that I smoked meth. What I didn't fully think through before I began this chase was that I was going to have to do more and more of this drug to get that feeling again and to maintain it. It became something I did every weekend, and I would lose myself for days on end, doing nothing but smoking meth, meth, and more meth.

Every time, the first hit was intense, and that intensity lasted minutes. Even after the intensity faded, the high continued on for hours and hours, lasting longer than any drug I'd ever used before. It kept me in this vicious cycle for days at a time. I would look up and realize twenty-four ... forty-eight ... seventy-two hours had passed by. I hadn't eaten, showered, or communicated with the outside world at all. The come down was the worst part, because I didn't want to be sober. I wanted to live my life in this perpetually high state of being.

I slowly became uninterested in living a double life. I no longer wanted to live two different lifestyles separately, simultaneously, and secretly. I just wanted to abandon reality and live in this drug world, in this euphoric la-la land, forever.

But at the same time, I didn't want that. There was always something in me that knew I couldn't continue in this way for the rest of my life. There was always that knowing in my knower that what I was doing was wrong. That I was better than the choices I was making. But I'd fallen so deep into this pool of sin that I figured it was easier to just keep swimming in the pool than it would be to attempt to climb out.

Isn't it wild how two conflicting desires can be so present in a person? I didn't know then what I know now about the flesh and the Spirit. My flesh, this sin nature etched into my being from birth, was bent toward evil. This sin nature craved bad, because bad feels good to the flesh. My flesh had desires that waged war against my soul. It was like Paul talks about in Romans chapter seven. There is no good in our sinful nature. I felt like even when I wanted to do what was right, I couldn't. Even though I had this slight desire to do what was good, I couldn't carry it out. I didn't want to do what was wrong, but I did it anyway.

Deep down, I was a wretched, unhappy person. And I was okay with being that way for years. I hadn't asked the question in Romans 7:24 yet. I hadn't inquired about *"Who will rescue me from this body that is subject to death?"* Because I wanted to be rescued, but not as much as I wanted to be high. I wasn't yet desperate enough to chase Jesus, but I was desperate enough to chase the dragon.

In hindsight, I see once again where the kindness of God kept me from death. So many times, I should have overdosed. So many times, I put myself in dangerous and life-threatening situations. I look back and ask myself, "What in the world was I thinking?" And that's just it. I wasn't thinking at all.

I lost myself on meth binges, slept with so many strangers, and smoked meth out of everything from glass pipes to aluminum foil to light bulbs. For five months straight.

When I came home from staying at meth houses, I felt like a zombie inside. I'd begun to look outwardly how I felt inwardly. My cheeks and eyes were all sunken. My hip bones and collar bones stuck out. The worst part of my appearance was the meth sores. With the cocaine and the pills, I could somewhat cover up how bad off I really was. But with the meth, there was no hiding the scabs all over my face.

I remember that Christmas, just a couple weeks after my first time doing meth, I looked like I had the chickenpox, but they were secluded to my cheeks and forehead, the result of me getting "lost in the mirror." I distinctly remember standing in front of the bathroom mirror for hours, picking at invisible bumps on my face. There wasn't anything there, but meth provides a mirage. I had two pimples on my face when I started picking, and by the time I was done, I had about fifty little bumps all over my face from where I had dug into my skin and made myself bleed.

When I left that meth house, I went home to my parents on Christmas Eve, and my dad asked me what was all over my face. I can't remember the lie I told him, but I do remember the disappointment on his face. He left home and returned with some Dr. Bronner's Tea Tree soap and cornstarch. Mixing the two together made a paste for acne-prone faces. He helped me make a paste for my scabs, and it significantly reduced the bumps.

On Christmas Day, when all of our family came over to open gifts, I was embarrassed and ashamed.

I have never forgotten my dad getting me that face soap. He

knew I was wrong. He knew I was lying and hiding something from him and my mom. He called me out on it. Yet after he called me out, he covered my shame. And I have never forgotten how he covered me in that way.

Have you ever read in Genesis chapter three, when God made clothes out of animal skins for Adam and Eve? Even though they sinned. Even though they were wrong. Even though they disobeyed God, then ran and hid from Him. He called for them anyway. "Where are you?" He asked them. He then told them the consequences of their actions. But after that, He made garments out of animal skin for them, and He clothed them.

He is still that way today, ya know? He still wants to walk with us in the cool of the day. He doesn't want us to run and hide from Him and try to cover our own shame or figure things out on our own. He is still calling out to you and me, asking, "Where are you?" He wants us to come out of hiding, confess our sins, and allow Him to clothe us in the garments of Christ.

He is still covering His kids' shame. But now, instead of repeatedly killing animals and covering us with animal skins as a sacrifice for our sins, He sees the sacrificial blood of Jesus covering us. He loves us so much that He allowed Jesus to die the death that we deserve. We get to be covered by the blood of Jesus, which purifies us from all sin.

When Jesus died on the cross, He covered us. He offered forever one sacrifice for all sin, then He sat at the right hand of God in heaven. Isn't it great that we don't have to try to sew together fig leaves to cover our own nakedness? Sacrifice for sin isn't necessary anymore when we receive what Jesus did on the cross. *He* is the sacrifice for sin.

If you don't know Jesus, or if you just want to know Him more, I pray right now that your eyes be opened and that you come to realize your own nakedness. I pray for an uncovering and an exposing of your own sin. That you receive the love of God, the covering of God, and the blood of Jesus, which has the power to cleanse your conscience and save your soul.

The irony of me praying this way for you right now is that I had no idea about the power of God to save, set free, and deliver back then. I thought that these scriptures only applied to other people and that the Bible stories that I had heard as a kid were only just that, Bible stories. I had no clue then that one day I would have my own story laced with supernatural miracles. Because at this point in my life, all I could see was a scar-faced addict in the mirror. And my earthly dad was trying to help me cleanse my face, while my heavenly Dad was concerned with cleansing my soul.

D ear reader, I can't end this chapter without a mini praise break:

Today, twelve years later, Carissa and her husband, who I mentioned in this chapter, are now both clean and sober and serving Jesus with their two kiddos. Ain't God good?

# CHAPTER 12
# GET-OUT-OF-JAIL FREE CARD

I wore a thousand faces of deceit, all offering a smile
to mask the storms within.

Since I lived at home, I was back to having to hide the depth of my addictions. I was at the mercy of my parents, my PTI officer, and my substance abuse rehab counselor.

Remember those charges I caught for the pills and drug paraphernalia? Well, most states have a program called Pre-trial Intervention, also known as PTI. PTI is similar to a second chance program. It's your one free bite out of the apple. A judge is allowed to grant first-time criminal offenders the option of doing PTI instead of probation. With PTI comes the opportunity to have the crimes you were charged with removed from your record. This comes with a series of stipulations and conditions you must meet, or you'll be kicked out of the program, your case will be sent back to court, and you'll have to reappear before a judge.

When I showed up at my court date and the public defender

that had been granted to me told me PTI was even an option, I was shocked, because I didn't know such a program existed. I stood before the judge and plead guilty to possession of controlled substances (the pills) with intent to distribute and possession of drug paraphernalia. The judge sentenced me to pre-trial intervention, which included forty hours of community service, weekly drug tests, and mandatory outpatient rehab classes.

Deceiving and being deceived, I continued forward in my manipulative ways, making everyone think that I wasn't as bad off as I really was. I mean, after all, I was back in school full time, even overtime. I was living at my parents' house, not out running the streets twenty-four-seven. I was going to rehab, so that meant I was clean and sober, right? *Wrong.*

The problem with this particular rehab was that I had the liberty to come and go. They saw me every Tuesday evening for one hour. They would have me pee in a little cup to check my urine for drugs, then they'd talk to us for thirty minutes about why drugs are bad, and that was it. Class was over, and they'd send me home with a piece of paper that had some facts on it, which of course found its way into the nearest trashcan every time.

For this very reason, now being on the other side of addiction, I'm not a huge proponent for outpatient rehabilitation programs. They have their place, but I feel like they don't hold enough space and time for people who are fresh out of addiction or who are still in active addiction to get serious about their recovery. The other problem with these outpatient programs is that people are often court ordered to attend them. Court-ordered mandates for short-term rehabs may not always help active addicts get clean long term. Court-ordered mandates may provide brief, seemingly instant behavioral modifications but don't always bring lasting results.

So, I attended this weekly group rehab therapy, checked the box on my sheet to say that I went, and then I would go right back out, that same night after class, to snort cocaine once again.

I still passed all of my drug tests, because both cocaine and meth only stay in your pee for about three to four days. I knew that as long as I stuck to drinking alcohol and doing drugs that I could get out of my system within seventy-two hours, I would be able to pass and clear my drug tests every Tuesday. Because I passed a weekly drug test, everyone assumed I wasn't doing drugs. No one really understood how bad addiction had a hold on me. This rehab didn't help me stop doing drugs; it helped me be more strategic about when and how I did them.

On top of PTI, per court order, I had to attend weekly Narcotics Anonymous (NA) meetings. Narcotics and Alcoholics Anonymous are global communities that are multilingual and multicultural with millions of participants. AA was founded in 1935 and is now in 180 countries.[1] NA was founded in 1953, and today its members hold over 70,000 meetings weekly in 144 countries.[2] AA is geared toward helping people in alcohol addiction, while NA is geared toward helping people in substance addiction, including but not limited to alcohol. The culture of these meetings is incredibly accepting and welcoming. Both pursue to be judgment free zones.

These are two of the most powerful communities in America, in my opinion. There are a few reasons why I feel this way. One, is that they are consistent and convenient, because you can find a meeting pretty much anytime, anywhere. Two, the leaders are loving. Three, the groups provide legit accountability. And four, participants are brutally honest about their struggles. Find a community like that, and it can be the biggest blessing ever, if you allow it to be.

Because of all the legal mess that I had gotten myself into, the judge ordered that I go to at least one of these meetings per week as part of my consequences for breaking the law. I had to get a paper signed every week by one of the meeting leaders that confirmed my attendance, which I would then submit to my PTI officer each time we met.

The organization has their own reading materials and principles that they follow called "The 12 Steps and the 12 Traditions."[3] The thing that stuck out to me the most at every meeting (I still remember it to this day) is tradition number three: "The only requirement for membership is a desire to stop using." That phrase can either frustrate a person or fill a person with hope. To the one who has no desire to stop using, it's like nails on a chalkboard, screeching in one ear and out the other. But to the one who has even an inkling of desire to stop using, it's like bells of joy, imparting hope.

At the start of each meeting, we'd read through different parts of the 12 Steps book, and every time I would hear the phrase "a desire to stop using," my insides cringed. I didn't have a desire to stop using. And I didn't want to be a member of this recovery group therapy session. I was there because I was told to be there. I was there because I could get in trouble with the law if I didn't follow the judge's orders. It was chill to be there, and I met some cool people along the way, but personally, I couldn't wait to get in and out of those meetings. That one hour couldn't go by quick enough. I was there to check a literal box on a piece of paper. A desire to stop using was the only requirement to be there, and I didn't even have that.

Sometimes, I went to these meetings on cocaine, the high lasting the whole duration of the meeting. Sometimes I went sober. One thing about being in these meetings is that I felt safe, I felt seen, and even though I never really shared my personal story, I felt heard. I felt safe and seen and heard because I saw myself in every person in that room. I heard my story in the stories they told, and it always felt good to hear of how they had overcome. I thought, *Wow, that was a good story. Good for them. Recovery is possible. But that's not for me. Maybe one day it will be for me. But today is not that day. And tomorrow isn't looking too good either.*

There's a difference between being court ordered to attend these meetings and attending them on your own accord. I truly believe that an addict will never get clean unless they want to get clean. Can one be motivated by outside forces? Sure. People, places, and opportunities can influence us to get clean, but at the end of the day, a person isn't going to stop using drugs for good until they themselves want to stop using drugs for good.

What is so hard about being an addict?

Being an addict is hard because addiction is the outward manifestation of inward issues. Often, deeply rooted inward issues. Painful inward issues. Unbearable inward issues.

Issues that started off as seeds. Maybe even seeds from childhood. Seeds of lies, abuse, trauma, rejection, or confusion. Seeds that eventually took root and grew into trees.

Being an addict is hard because you would rather numb the inward pain and escape reality than attempt to cut down the tree that's rotting inside of you. The longer you let that tree grow and the more you nurture it, the bigger it gets and the more it overtakes you as a person. It grows more limbs and produces more destructive fruit in your inward parts until it has completely overtaken your mind, your heart, your emotions, and your body. Until it has completely overtaken all that you care about. Until it has completely choked out any life, hope, or future you ever once dreamed of.

All you want is that drug that will make you forget about the massive, rotten, dark, aching places inside of you. What started off as a small seed of self-medication turns into an obsessive addiction that enslaves you.

A literal synonym for addiction is *enslavement*. Our addictions often become our idols. Our idols are our objects of worship. When we have a dependency on anything other than Jesus, that thing will always exalt itself to the place that only Jesus is meant to hold. That can be done with all sorts of things, including people, time, and resources.

In every human is a longing to belong. And when you don't

know where you belong, you search in different places until you find one that feels like home. I saw that in these meetings. It felt like home to the other members. Some had been going for days and others for decades. *Every day or every week for decades. Some of them traded their drug addiction for a meeting addiction.* But let's just admit that sometimes we do that. Sometimes we trade one addiction in for another "lesser" addiction. But I don't think we were meant to crave anything in such a way that we are a slave to it.

I see addiction as a form of idol worship. That type of craving, adoration, and obsession should be reserved for only One. Deep down, we all crave to be loved. Not realizing that we already are, forsaking the One who *is* Love in the process, we make our homes with other people in other places and pour our worship toward lifeless idols.

Week by week I attended the meetings, as well as the weekly outpatient rehabs, going through the motions. While crossing my *T*s and dotting my *I*s so that everything looked good on paper, inwardly I wasted away. I was in a dark place. I no longer had a hold on my addiction, but it had a hold on me, and its dark roots grew deeper and deeper.

2012 was the year of YOLO as I continued in this reckless living. My weeks went like this: meetings, rehab class, school, parties, clubs, drugs, sex, repeat.

I was also court ordered to do forty hours of community service. So, in my spare time, I completed twenty of those hours volunteering at a local Miracle Hill Thrift Store. Then, I decided I was done serving the community, and I forged signatures for the remaining twenty hours. On paper, I'd made it look like I was all done with my hours. I turned it in to my PTI officer, ready to be finished with these legal dealings and continue on with my life.

It turned out that my PTI officer was actually a pretty smart lady, and she found out that I had forged those hours. She kicked me out of the Pre-trial Intervention Program and sent my case back to court. After all my hard work of going through the motions for months, I'd flushed it down the toilet. And there went my get-out-of-jail free card with it.

When I reappeared before the judge, she told me she could prosecute and charge me again, adding an additional offense—lying on a government document. Thankfully, she didn't. (Peep the mercy of God in my life, yet again.) She doubled my community service hours and sentenced me to one year on probation, as well as to complete yet another outpatient rehab program.

These outpatient rehabs didn't help me stop doing drugs. But in a way, they were a keeper to me. They acted as a buffer—not stopping but slightly slowing down my rapid decline. Knowing that I was going to get drug tested every week, and that if I failed a drug test I could be put in jail, put a healthy fear in me. And that truly kept me. Because even though I wanted to do hard drugs every single day, I was forced to reduce my habits to only a couple of days out of the week.

Believe it or not, I graduated in June 2012. Only by the grace of God, I walked across that stage and received my high school diploma with my graduating class. I was so dang proud of myself. That was a happy day. A good day.

It's a miracle that I was able to graduate high school, considering the life that I was living. Even though I'd dropped out just a year prior, I went back and re-enrolled, put in the time, and worked my butt off to walk that stage. This is why it's important not to judge a book by its cover.

It's important that we truly be able to discern what people are going through. Ninety-eight percent of the people in my school and in my life had no idea how bad my addiction was. They had no idea that I was selling my body for drugs, snorting pills, smoking meth, and had a baggie of cocaine in my wallet at all times. They just thought I was your average, rebellious teenage girl who smoked a little weed, drank a little alcohol, and skipped school on occasion. But it was so much bigger than that. It's *always* so much bigger than that.

Just like I mentioned in the "Gateway" chapter, you think it'll never be you or your child or your spouse or your sibling … until it is. Addiction is no respecter of persons. Addicts can be people of great achievements, accolades, and accomplishments. We must learn to see past the outward appearance of a person and into their heart, because that is where we discover who they really are. And what they're really made of.

# CHAPTER 13

# SELLING MYSELF SHORT AT A BREASTAURANT

My life is a picture of how one tiny compromise after another will take you in a handbasket straight down into the pit of hell.

When I graduated from Eastside High School, I had no clue what to do next. My life the summer that followed was really no different than the life I'd already been living. Except now I had more free time to go to parties and clubs and to get high and sleep around.

I was going to need a job, and I heard there was a new sports bar opening in August, so I went and put in my application and was hired on the spot. As an eighteen-year-old girl, I was super excited to be hired at a place where I could dress up, accessorize, and do my hair and makeup every day.

But this wasn't your typical sports bar that sold wings and booze. No, this bar sold more than food and beer. It sold sex appeal and an experience built on allure and attraction. If you've never heard of breastaurants before, they're basically risqué restaurants that profit from the objectification of women. Places where female sexuality is commercialized through suggestive entertainment. And while people may not be having literal sex within the four walls of the actual building, these establishments act as a middleman. They've found a loophole through which they can legally operate and be a sort of watering hole where predators come to find their prey. They cut out the hard work for the sexual consumer and supply the demand of beautiful young women in abundance.

You may be tempted to envision a certain type of person when you think about who these sexual consumers could be. But just like I said in chapter six about addiction, perversion attempts to seduce everyone. Young or old, male or female, doctor, dentist, teacher, or waitress. Pastor, neighbor, friend, policeman, firefighter, or politician. Lay aside every preconception, because sexual consumers are all around us, even right in front of our very faces.

I still remember the first day of training, when they brought us in and talked to us about how they expected us to come to work. We were expected to show up to work at 10AM every morning in a clean uniform. *That's reasonable.* Our khaki booty shorts and skintight, crop-top shirts had to be clean. *Got it.* Knee-high socks with winter boots. *Okay, socks and shoes. Got it.* Our hair was not allowed to be in a ponytail or a bun, only down. This seemed strange, because in most food industries you're required to wear your hair pulled up or to wear some sort of hair net. *But okay, got it.* We were required to wear jewelry, but not just any jewelry. "Bling" jewelry. Earrings, necklace, bracelets, rings, all of it. And lastly, we were expected to show up with a full face of makeup: foundation, bronzer, blush, eyeshadow, eyeliner, mascara, and lipstick. The whole shebang. And we got bonus points if our nails were painted.

We were introduced to their ranking system, which was used to give select employees seniority. It's used to pick which sections of tables we got to wait on, to decide who got to leave work early, and who got certain days off. Rank was determined by a bunch of different things, like being on time and teamwork, but mostly it was based on physical appearance. Oh, and while not officially part of the criteria, it was clear that having a closer relationship with one of the managers would surely find you favor on the rank chart too. It was basically a strip club without the stripping. The restaurant had decent-tasting food and ice-cold, 29-degree draft beer, but let's be real. No one goes there for the food and beer. And if you say that's why you go there, then go ahead and repent for lying.

I was fresh out of high school and very naïve. I already used my body to get the guys and the drugs that I wanted, so what more was dressing half naked and getting paid to walk around and serve food to people? Sounded dreamy to me.

I didn't understand then that normalizing the sexualization of women is wrong. This industry preys on girls like me, glorifying the sexual exploitation of our bodies and presenting it as a wonderful opportunity that they've wrapped up in a big red bow. I didn't understand that my body had value. Remember, my childhood dream was to grow up to be a porn star. In my mind, a woman was to use her body to get whatever she wanted, just like peanut butter goes with jelly on a sandwich. It was just what women did. To me, that was truly my perspective of how I was to use my body. And so that's what I began to do.

Almost every day and night for over a year, I worked as one of their girls. This was where I learned to perfect my craft. They trained us in this very thing. We were coached on how to sit down with our tables all throughout their dining experience. And while we were sitting, we were taught to implement the 3 S's. Sit. Schmooze. Sell. Sit with the customer, schmooze (a.k.a. flirt with) the customer, and up-sell the customer by offering extra drinks, dessert, or merchandise. They not only encouraged me, they lowkey taught me how to manipulate men, and in my brain every customer was my victim. I would schmooze them every which way I needed to in order squeeze the most money out of them.

The money was good, and no one cared if I was high at work, as long as I could still do my job. I would even sneak out to my car on my cigarette break to get high. It was a good job for an addict, and for me, it was fun.

One day, a single, black man dressed in a suit came and sat in my section. Twelve years later, I still remember his order. He always wanted grilled tilapia and a side of mixed veggies with an OJ and Tanqueray, salt on the rim. One conversation led to another then to another. When he left, I found a hundred-dollar tip on the table. He became a regular of mine and would leave me that tip every time.

Finally, one day he asked if I would meet him after work and promised me more money if I did. I didn't know fully what he expected of me, but I said, "Sure."

Mind you, I was eighteen years old, and this man was old

enough to be my dad. A lot of our regulars that frequented the restaurant were older, married men.

When he gave me a couple extra hundred dollars and told me to buy myself a sexy outfit before coming, I knew what was expected of me. By then, I had already made up my mind that I'd move forward with the plan when the time came to do so.

We met at one of his many houses, and he asked me to dance for him. I never got fully undressed, and we never did anything, not even so much as a kiss. But I danced in front of him, and he threw money at me like I was his own private stripper. When he was over it, he turned off the music, and I stopped. Degrading myself even further, I got down on my knees and collected those dollar bills off the ground, one by one, before I got dressed and headed out. This gave a whole new meaning to using my body to get what I wanted. And I was only just getting started.

At this point in my life, any bit of integrity that I had left was gone.

It hit me that the more I was willing to do, the more money I could make. I teamed up with girls who were older than me, and we went on double dates with these sugar daddies (a.k.a. married men, many of whom had children our age). We exchanged sexual favors for shopping sprees and a few hundred-dollar bills.

I put a two-hundred-dollar price tag on my body and sold it in full to whoever was willing to pay the price. After all, I had bills to pay and drugs to buy. I'd always have to be drunk—almost black-out, belligerent drunk—to do some of the unspeakable things that we did. I don't think I ever once did these things sober or in my right mind. I was so disgusted with myself and just wanted the sexual acts to hurry up and be over. For the most part, they never lasted too long, and I'd collect my payment and say my goodbyes.

A price tag cannot be placed on any human body. But, when you don't know your worth, you can end up selling yourself short by literally selling yourself. If only I knew that the value that I had to offer ran so much deeper than what meets the eye.

My YOLO motto led me more and more into dark and dusty places, but I never imagined that it would lead me to a breastaurant where I would learn to prostitute myself. And I never should've met a Greenville, SC state senator in a place like that. But it turns out he had a thing for half-naked women serving him OJ and Tanqueray.

Yep, that's right. The very man who introduced and launched me out into this lifestyle all the more was a Greenville County Senator. After that first meeting, he'd have me meet him at different strip clubs all over town, where we'd receive VIP access. There, he would hand me stacks of one-dollar bills by the hundreds and instruct me on how to throw the money at the dancers.

The more I got exposed to this world, the more I wanted to be a part of it. I didn't realize that I was actually being groomed and exploited by a wealthy and respected politician.

I didn't see it like this then, but it was as if the devil himself was taking me by the hand and step by step showing me what my life could be like if I continued down this slippery slope. If I continued to fully give over to the darkness that called me deeper. My heart was never fully hardened to the things of God, and Satan knew that. Yet still, it was like the devil was saying to me, "Look, you can make even more money. You can buy even nicer clothes. You can do even more drugs." It was an invitation into a lifestyle, beckoning me to go a little deeper and a little deeper and a little deeper until the waves of sin swallowed me whole and drowned me.

# CHAPTER 14
# THINGS BACK HOME

The more my world broke apart, the more I did too.

During all my sexual shenanigans outside the home, the devil kept himself busy tearing apart my family inside the home. While out running the streets most of the time, I didn't know, nor care to know, how bad things truly were at home. Around the time I began working at the breastaurant, in September of 2012, my mom got deathly sick. One morning she woke up completely paralyzed. Her brain worked and she could talk, but she'd lost all movement in her limbs. My younger brother, Holden, who was fourteen at the time, was the only one home that morning. When he found Mama in her bedroom, he immediately called 911.

The paramedics came and rushed Mama to Spartanburg Regional Hospital, where she spent the next seventeen days in a coma. Her pancreas had shut down, and they diagnosed her with severe acute Pancreatitis, which is a very painful condition where one's pancreas becomes super inflamed. The inflammation became so bad that it got infected, and the infection spread rapidly throughout her entire body. The hospital doctors didn't know how to treat her and called in specialists from around the country for extra opinions and help.

They eventually used Mama's rare situation as a case study, because they were all mind blown that she was even still alive. It made no sense. With the level of infection in her body, she should have been dead. She did flatline at one point during her hospital stay. When she was on the operating table, the doctors lost her heartbeat for about two minutes. During that time, she had a near-death experience that changed her life forever.

She said that she was sitting on the edge of God's hand—a hand bigger than the sky. Her legs dangled over the edge, and she was laughing and full of joy. She didn't have any pain, sadness, or depression. She wasn't thinking about her kids, her husband, her friends, or anyone else on earth. She was in a pure, blissful paradise. I am so thankful that she had this experience, but I'm even more thankful for what God spoke to her during this supernatural encounter. God told her that her work on earth wasn't finished yet and that she would live to see her children grow up into adulthood.

The doctors told Nanny (my mom's mom) that no one with this severe of a case of acute Pancreatitis had ever survived. But thank God for praying grandmas, because my nanny was not about to receive those doctors' words as gospel. She prayed for Mama's healing, and she started a prayer chain with other believers from all around the world. After two-and-a-half long weeks, Mama finally woke up out of her coma. But her road to healing had just begun.

Meanwhile, I lived in a perpetual state of absentmindedness, so consumed with myself that I had zero regard for anyone else. Not even my own mother. Mama was in the hospital fighting for her life while I was out in the streets selling my body for drugs. Her first stay in the hospital lasted for over a month. When they released her, she was able to come home for two short days before she was readmitted for another month-long stay. And for the entire duration of her two-plus months in the hospital, I can count on one hand the number of times that I went to visit her. This isn't my proudest moment, but this is the raw truth of what drug addiction does to people and to families. It chews you up and spits you out. And when you're in the midst of it, you don't even realize that it is slowly sucking the life out of you and out of every relationship that you have.

As my dad was busy doing his own thing, working through his own issues and working his full-time job, my younger sister and brother slipped through the cracks. My fourteen-year-old brother Holden and my sixteen-year-old sister Sydney began dabbling in things that teenagers sometimes dabble in, and I foolishly gave them my stamp of approval. I was the cool big sister. The one who would get them alcohol and weed. I still remember the first time that I made Holden and his friends a makeshift bong out of a water bottle and aluminum foil. I also helped Sydney dress up all provocative and sexy then proceeded to coach her on how to present herself to her boyfriend. I encouraged my siblings to rebel. I thank God that He kept my siblings from following my horrible influence headfirst into my footsteps.

Our white-picket-fence family had been torn apart. My parents separated. Daddy moved out and began a new relationship. Mama was still in recovery mode, healing from her time in the hospital. In March 2013, we were forced to move out of our house that my parents had built from the ground up. My parents' dream-come-true home. The place that held so many childhood and family memories. Mama and my siblings moved into an apartment. I moved into my own place with a friend.

When life as you've known it flips upside down, it almost always seems to happen suddenly. Suddenly, Mama was sick. Suddenly, my parents were getting divorced. Suddenly, our home was in foreclosure. Then suddenly, we got evicted.

It's hard to pick up the pieces of your life when everything feels so chaotic and broken. It's hard to move forward into the unknown. But sometimes that's what life forces us to do.

Everything happened so fast and was *so* beyond my control. I didn't know how to cope with my dysfunctional life, so I coped without even realizing that I was coping. I coped in the ways that I always did. Everything going on at home and with Mama was just another excuse to stay high. More problems I didn't want to deal with. More emotions I needed to numb. But my coping really wasn't coping at all. It was more like self-medicating. Treating my surface wounds but never willing or ready to attack the root of my own spiritual sickness.

But hey, I was grown now. Legally, I was an adult. I was moving into my very first apartment, and no one could tell me nothin'. I was old enough to make adult decisions, but not responsible enough to steward those decisions. Let me note that there is a difference between being an adult and being a *responsible* adult. I don't believe that anyone on drugs is truly capable of being responsible. Drug addicts cannot be trusted to make rational, level-headed decisions on a consistent basis. Why? Because drug addicts are on a continual roller coaster, up one day and down the next. The only thing I was able to be consistent in was getting high.

# CHAPTER 15
# THE POWER OF THE TONGUE

Whoever said, "Sticks and stones may break my bones,
but words will never hurt me," lied.

As I'm sure you can imagine, my new townhouse quickly turned into a community dope house. It had no decorations and was empty of life, color, and character. I didn't have a TV. Not even a couch to sit on. I rarely had food in the cabinets or drinks in the fridge. But what I did have was weed, cigarillos, alcohol, pills, cocaine, and all the drug paraphernalia that I needed. Addiction was my entire identity. I lived to smoke and smoked to live. Sex, drugs, money, sex, drugs, money, repeat. I had different partners every week. Sometimes every day. I cannot count on all my fingers and toes the number of people I slept with. It became all that I knew. My consistent normal. My way of living.

But around April 20, 2013, everything changed. I remember it so vividly because April 20th is the unofficial National Marijuana Holiday, a day known to all pot smokers as a day to celebrate smoking pot. Me and my three friends went into Whatever

3, a local body piercing shop that sells jewelry, glass bowls, and other random items. And that's when I saw him. Michael. This tall, olive-skinned man with high cheekbones and long, black hair. He was half Asian, half white, and much older than me. Handsome. Better yet, *beautiful*.

But why did he look so angry?

The girls and I shopped around for awhile, and before we left, I tried to hit on him. At first, he denied me, saying I was way too young for him. I assured him that I was of legal age. He still denied me, saying that he had sisters my age. But I wouldn't take no for an answer. Before we walked out of the store, I wrote my phone number down on a yellow sticky note and stuck it onto the cash register. I had no clue if he would do anything with that little sticky note, but later that evening I got that first text message:

Hey beautiful :)

And so, it began.

A couple days of back-and-forth texting happened. Then, he invited me over to his place to smoke. I drove to this complete stranger's house, and we hung out all night. And again, the next night and the next night and the next night. Between our instant chemistry and his endless supply of drugs (Yay for me!), there really was no reason for me to go back to my newly rented apartment. And so, I didn't. As fate would have it, my housemate and I ended up getting into a huge fight—so huge it ended our friendship—right around this same time. We broke our lease, and I moved in with Michael. After knowing this man for two weeks, I left all that I had at the apartment and never looked back.

After all those years of looking for love in all the wrong places, I thought maybe I had found my happily ever after, after all. But the strange thing was that our relationship wasn't all that happy. When we were good, we were great. But when we were bad, we were horrible. There was no middle ground. We were at our happiest together if we were high. Otherwise, we didn't trust each other. We constantly fought, argued, and cussed each other out. It didn't take long for me to realize why he looked so angry in the piercing shop that day.

I had been in abusive relationships before. I had dealt with being emotionally manipulated and verbally mistreated before. I had even been hit and smacked across the face before, but this man carried a different type of pain and anger deep in his heart, and if you triggered him even slightly, you unleashed the beast. Especially if he was sober.

That's what happens when a person becomes addicted to substances. Drugs change people, and they become another person than who they were truly created to be. Michael was so dependent on the drugs that he would have extreme mood swings when he wasn't on them. Michael wasn't a bad man; he was a hurting man. That's one thing I have come to realize about people in addiction. Most people who struggle with addiction have abuse, rejection, self-hatred, or other deep-seated pain that hasn't been dealt with. At the end of the day, Michael and I were really no different. His pain manifested as anger, while my pain manifested as promiscuity. Both led us to being addicts.

Needless to say, our relationship was super toxic. We basically broke up and then got right back together every single day. But one day, we got into our biggest fight ever. I don't even remember what this particular fight was about. But I do remember that we were going back and forth and cussing each other out when he screamed, "I hate my life! I hope I crash my bike, and I hope I die!"

I was shocked he would verbalize something like that, and I quickly spewed back, "Don't say stuff like that! Your words are powerful! Don't ever say that!"

The fight continued, and he ended up leaving the house, speeding off angrily on his motorcycle. I thought that this was just like all of our other fights. I thought that he just needed some time to cool down and then we would make up a few hours later and everything would be back to normal. But hours passed, and I still hadn't heard anything from him.

The day turned into night, and I needed to numb my pain, like I always did, so I got drunk. In fact, I got so drunk that I couldn't drive home to Michael's, and I spent the night with Carly and Titi. We all had to be at work at the breastaurant at 10AM the next morning. I figured I'd work all day and then go back home to Michael's so that we could make up and be back to normal.

But around lunchtime, I got a phone call at work. I went up to the hostess stand and answered the business landline. I fingered the curly, black, rubber cord and put the phone to my ear, confused and thinking, *who would be calling me at work? What could be this urgent?*

It was my friend Dori. "Hey Babe, did you know that Mike was in a motorcycle accident last night?"

My heart sank. I had no idea. My mind and imagination instantly flooded with worst-case scenarios. I told my boss that I needed to leave immediately because my boyfriend had been hit on his motorcycle. A friend from work drove me to Greenville Memorial hospital.

I had never before felt so much adrenaline, fear, sadness, and anxiety pumping through my body all at once. Shaking and scared, I didn't know what to expect. I didn't know what was going on. I was fully sober in this moment, but I felt incoherent. I couldn't think or talk straight. All I wanted was to see Michael. All I wanted to do was hug him and hear him tell me that we were good and that everything was going to be okay.

When we arrived, I ran through the large, golden, spinning doors of the hospital and got on the elevator to ride up to the third floor. Full of worry and fear, I exited the elevator and trembled as I walked up to a woman sitting behind a computer. I told her that I needed to see my boyfriend, Michael Cline, only to be met with the rejection of her telling me that she couldn't let me back into ICU without his family's permission.

*But all his family lived out of state.*

I had no other option but to sit in the waiting room and wait for my opportunity to sneak through the automatic, locked doors that lead back to the ICU rooms. When I saw my open door (literally), I slid past the lady at the computer and ran around the corner to look for Michael.

After a minute or so, I found him lying in a bed. What I saw shook me to my core. I can still smell the stale hospital room and hear all the loud, beeping machines in the quiet of the ICU. Michael was swollen, his head was wrapped in bandages, and he had all sorts of tubes and wires and needles in him.

A nurse came around the corner, and I asked her, "Is he going to be okay?"

"Honey, he's brain-dead. It will be up to his family to decide whether they will keep him on this ventilator or not," she replied.

Shocked and stunned, I walked out and sat alone in the waiting room and wept. In that moment, I didn't know what to do. I felt so helpless. Helpless, but interestingly enough, not hopeless.

As I sat in that waiting room, I began to think about my only hope. I began to think about God. I recalled going to church as a little girl and all these different bible stories flooded my mind. With tears streaming down my face, I said, "God! I don't know what else to do, so I'm coming to You. God! I remember being a little kid. I remember hearing stories of how You healed people, of how You opened blind eyes, of how You opened deaf ears, of how You raised the dead. If that's true … if You are real … then *heal him*! Heal Michael! Please! I'm begging You to heal him and to raise him up. If You do this, then I will give my life to You. And I'll make Michael give his life to You too. We will serve You, all the days of our life. If You heal him."

For the next seventy-two hours, I did not leave those hospital grounds. Titi and Carly dropped off food, clothes, and pre-rolled blunts for me. I would sneak out and smoke and come right back into the ICU unit. I didn't want to leave. I couldn't leave. I had to be there for when God raised him from the dead. I had to be there for when the doctors came in and exclaimed, "It's unexplainable. A miracle has taken place."

Ever since I was a little girl, I'd always believed in the power of prayer. Even as I grew older, in some of my darkest moments and deepest pain, I would talk to God. Mostly when I needed something from Him. But I have always believed that God answers prayer. I truly did believe with all my heart that God was going to heal Michael, and I prayed harder for his healing than anything I had ever prayed for in my entire life.

I asked every person I came in contact with to join with me in praying. From the doctors to the nurses to the cafeteria workers to random people coming to visit their own loved ones. I would ask them, "Do you believe in God? Do you believe that He can do miracles?" And if they said yes, then I would share Michael's story with them. "My boyfriend got into a motorcycle accident. He is currently brain-dead, and he's in ICU on a ventilator. Will you join me in prayer? Will you join me in believing that God is going to heal him, that God is going to raise him up?" And I prayed with hundreds of strangers, knowing that Michael's healing would be one of those stories that only God could get the glory from.

His family had driven up from Georgia, and after three long days, they made the decision to take him off the ventilator. When they told me their decision, my heart ached with a pain that I had never felt before. Why would they take him off? Why would they not leave him on a little longer and believe for a miracle of God to take place? Why were they giving up on him? Why were they letting him go? I had so many questions that I dared not vocalize. I wasn't his wife. I wasn't family. They didn't know me from Eve. For all they knew, I was some random girl off the street. So, I respected their decision. And beyond my control, unceasing tears poured out of my eyes and flooded down my cheeks.

As a total stranger to them, I am forever thankful that they held space for me, Carly, and Titi to go in and say our goodbyes to Michael before they pulled the plug on him. We went in and stood over his dying body.

I grabbed his swollen fingers, and I felt him twitch. The nurse assured me that it was just a bodily reaction and that he was mentally gone. The machine was the only thing keeping his heart pumping.

I ignored her. In my brain, if his heart was still pumping and he was still breathing, then he was still living, machine or not. I snapped back, "They say that hearing is the last thing to go, and I believe that he can still hear me."

And with that belief in my heart, I said, "Hey Babe, in just a little bit, they are going to unplug this machine from you, and you are going to die. Don't be afraid. You don't have to be afraid. If you pray this prayer with me, then you will go to heaven when you die. The Bible says that if you believe in your heart and confess with your mouth that Jesus died on the cross for your sins, then you will be saved. So, repeat after me." Then I led him in prayer. "God, I know that I am a sinner, and I have sinned against You, and I'm sorry. I believe that Jesus died on the cross for my sins, and I want to accept Him as my Savior. Amen."

I kissed his swollen, chapped lips and bent down to hug his tense, stiff body. He smelled like petroleum jelly and hospital sheets. Such a distinct smell. Then I walked out of that room, slid down the wall, sat on the cold tile of the hospital floor, and buried my face in my hands as I wept and groaned in agony.

Titi said she was going to get the car and drive around to pick me up at the front of the building. She told me to take my time. And I did.

# CHAPTER 16
## A BROKEN HALLELUJAH

*Surrender is to trust that in losing our lives we actually find our lives.*

Anxiety and grief filled my body like I had never felt before. After a few minutes, I rode down the elevator, opened a heavy oak door, and about ten empty bathroom stalls stood before me. I walked halfway down then turned to my left and flung open one of the stall doors.

I thought I was going to be angry at God. I thought I was going to point my finger at Him and say, "You're not real!" But instead, the opposite happened. This tragedy had removed the scales from my eyes, and thoughts of eternity overwhelmed me. I closed and locked the door to that bathroom stall, and I fell down on my knees and word vomited toward heaven, "God, I am so sorry! I realize now that I could have been on that motorcycle with Michael. That could have been me that died. I don't want to live this way anymore. Take my life and use it for Your glory."

In that very moment, I had an epiphany that demanded a response. God had spared my life, and I had never felt more certain of the fact that He was real, He was present, and He loved me very much.

As I repented, I felt demons digging their claws into my shoulders on each side of my body. They didn't want to let go, but I could physically feel their claws being ripped out of me. In a single moment of surrender and repentance, the demonic grip of Satan was broken off of my life. I could physically feel the darkness being lifted off of me. Simultaneously, I felt totally overcome by peace. Like an invisible blanket had dropped down from the ceiling and landed on top of me. There I was on my knees, covered and cloaked in this heavy peace. I didn't know then, but now I know, that was the Holy Spirit.

I met the Holy Spirit on the cold, hard, bathroom floor of Greenville Memorial Hospital. There was no pastor present. No one walked me through the sinner's prayer. No one called me down to an altar and laid hands on me. There was no Bible, no anointing oil, and no worship team in the background playing gentle music. It was Jesus Himself in the person of the Holy Spirit who touched me and set me free. I was instantly delivered from years of demonization. Instantly born again. Instantly made new.

I didn't understand it all at first. The love of my life had just died suddenly. I should've been dying inside. I should've been so broken and distraught. I should've run to every drug I could possibly get my hands on so that I didn't have to experience the pain of my loss. But I didn't. I didn't want to numb my pain in that way anymore. I didn't want to drink my pain away. Don't get me wrong, I had a broken heart and felt deep sadness, but despite that reality, I had this peace that transcends human understanding.

I like to use the analogy of a lightbulb. You know how light bulbs are made of thin glass? They are fragile, and you can hold them in the palm of your hand. But if you were to pick up a lightbulb, draw back your arm, and throw it as hard as you possibly could at a brick wall, what would happen to that lightbulb? It would shatter into a million pieces, right?

My heart felt like a lightbulb in the palm of my hands, and losing Michael felt like I was throwing my lightbulb heart as hard as I possibly could at a brick wall. But instead of shattering into a million pieces, my lightbulb heart hit the wall, fell to the ground, bounced gently a couple of times, then rolled around a little until coming to a complete stop. It didn't shatter. It wasn't destroyed beyond repair. It *felt* like it was shattering, but it wasn't. God was holding my heart through the throwing, the dropping, the bouncing, and the rolling. He was holding it, and He was keeping it in one piece.

Normally I would have run straight to the nearest bar to drown myself in tequila, but to my own surprise, I didn't want to do that. I walked out of the hospital, climbed into the car and told Titi, "This is weird… but I don't even have a desire to drink. Can you just take me to my mom's house?"

Before we pulled out of the parking lot, I called my mom, briefly explained to her what had happened, and asked her if I could move back home. Once again, she took me in with open arms and loved me right where I was at.

I took a month off of work, and all I did was smoke weed on my mom's front porch, sleep, and write in my journal. Ever since I was a little girl, I have enjoyed writing. I had random notebooks filled with stories, poetry, and "dear God" letters, where I would write out my prayers. I even had one of those old-school "girl tech password journals," the kind that were voice activated, and you had to record your own password to get it to open. #90sbaby. In elementary school, I'd received a governor's writing award.

Writing has always come naturally to me and has been a source of joy throughout my life. So, when Michael died, I went back to my roots and began journaling again. There's scientific evidence supporting the therapeutic and healing power of writing. Research by James Pennebaker in 1986 showed that expressive writing—where we pour out our deepest thoughts and feelings—can lead to profound physical and psychological benefits. His studies revealed improvements like better immune function, lower blood pressure, reduced anxiety and depression, and a happier mood.[1] Writing helped me to grieve and process the loss of Michael, and it continues to help me process and work through things today.

I still have the first journal I started twelve years ago. Below is my very first journal entry in the days that followed Michael's passing:

Sept. 9, 2013 11:35 PM
So, I'm not really sure where to begin. But I figure I should begin soon, somewhere.
My mind is so blank and sometimes I feel so empty and hollow.
My life has by no means been an easy one, but it's definitely been worthy.
As of right now, I feel at a crossroad. I feel at war within myself and at war with the devil. All of me wants to live for Jesus because I've come to the realization and conclusion that this world has nothing for me. That truly when you think about it, 100 years from now all that will matter is who was saved and who wasn't. I do not want to get left behind and I know that I must change my ways.
I am praying for the strength to carry on, for in this moment, I am broken. My heart aches as I

force a smile upon my face every day, but I keep going because I know that soon there's gonna be a brighter day. I thank God each day I wake up for letting me be so blessed with wisdom. If there's one thing no one can take from me, it is my knowledge, for I know that I am wise beyond my years. I know that I am talented, that I have a gift that I must figure out how to use. Which to me is the hard part. To be honest, I'm quite scared to screw up. "To those which much is given, much is also expected."

I feel like a part of me died and went to Heaven w/ him, as well as a part of him lives in me. 20 years old w/out a clue of what to do or where to go. Life continues on around me and I realize that there's really not more to life than this.

I mean, honestly, we were put here for one reason, and that reason is to live for Jesus, because He died for our sin, and to spread the word of the Lord that we might rescue people from the evil, corrupt ways of the diegetic world, of the devil. Satan has a way of coming for those who refuse him. Look at Job. In the Bible. The devil hates it when we give thanks and praise to the Lord, and I know he is trying to stop me in every way in his power. But I will not be moved. When I give into the temptations of the devil I feel guilty and dirty. I know that the Lord will forgive me of my

*unpure thoughts and actions, but it hurts to know
I've disappointed him ...
I am my own worst critic, so hard on myself b/c
who else is going to be. I have somewhat mastered
the virtue of patience, but for some reason I'm
struggling w/ addiction, forgiveness and lettin' go.*

LOL at twenty-year-old me who thought that she had "mastered the virtue of patience!" That's funny.

But *wow*. So many emotions in one journal entry.

Before I had even read a single word in the Bible, the Lord was working in me. I had no clue about the wrestle that Paul describes in Romans chapter seven. My spirit had instantly been born again in that bathroom stall, but my flesh still screamed out for what it had always known. My body cried out against my new, born-again self. As a baby Christian, not even one month old in the Lord, I could sense the very real spiritual war that was taking place over my soul. I had been the enemy's soldier in his camp of sin and darkness for so long that he wasn't willing to just let me slip away without a fight. My salvation was a done deal, but the enemy still held out hope that I wouldn't leave his camp completely. I was faithful in the kingdom of darkness, bold about my life of sin, and a leader that brought others along with me into evil. The devil wasn't happy to see me go.

But God hadn't met me the night that Michael died for nothing. He'd met me in the pit of hell, but He didn't leave me there. He'd met me in deep, deep brokenness, but He didn't leave me there. He'd met me in a state of active drug addiction, but He didn't leave me there.

With God's extravagant love, He met me where I was at, but He didn't leave me where He found me. He called me up. He called me higher.

I believe that as He called me, He thought to Himself, "Once I put My Spirit on the inside of her, she will be new inside, she will be holy inside, she will be Mine."

He knew it would take time before what was going on inside of me began to bleed out of my heart and into my everyday life, but He took that chance with me.

He said "yes" to me long before I ever said "yes" to Him.

# CHAPTER 17
# NEW START MINISTRY

The Lord had led my family and I to New Start Ministry.
It was time for just that. A new start.

After about a week of living back at my mom's house, she asked me if I wanted to go to church with her and my younger siblings. Mama, my younger sister Sydney, and my younger brother Holden had started going to this church just a few months prior. Isn't it amazing how God orchestrates our lives and intertwines them so brilliantly with the lives of others? God is a genius. He had already been working and drawing my family to Himself. Next up on His agenda: bring the prodigal daughter home.

"Sure, I'll go. I need God in my life."

I was willing to go to church with them, but only under one condition: I could smoke weed beforehand. I didn't do anything in my life without getting high first, and church wasn't going to be an exception.

Sunday rolled around, and I asked Sydney for an appropriate

dress to wear, because all I owned were tube tops, mini dresses, stripper stilettos, and club clothes.

At 11AM, we loaded into Mama's car and drove about ten minutes down the road. We pulled into the parking lot of an old, brick, elementary school building with a sign in the yard that read "New Start Ministry."

As we went inside, I'll never forget how we were so warmly welcomed with overwhelming love. It was nice to feel welcomed, seen, and accepted. But I wasn't entirely trusting of others yet. *Hmm, this has got to be too good to be true.* I didn't talk much that first time visiting New Start Ministry, which is very unlike me because I almost always have something to say. Instead, I sat back and took it all in. I watched the people around me and wondered, *is this all real? Are these people genuine? They are all so nice.*

I guess the reason their kindness shocked me so much was because floating around in the back of my head, I had this thought that Christian people were boring, hypocritical, judgmental, and fake. I enjoyed being there but told myself I would need to come back a second time to see if this whole thing was really legit.

So, I came back the following Thursday for Bible study. This evening, I came straight from work at the breastaurant, so I walked inside wearing my uniform. I had on snow boots, booty shorts, and a T-shirt in the mid-August, South Carolina heat. I wasn't dressed for church, and once again, I showed up high. Yet, once again, I was met with such compassion, love, and acceptance. I sensed their genuineness and that they really wanted me to be there.

Another Sunday service, same thing. Another Bible study, same thing. It was real, and I liked it there. I felt safe and free. These people who I thought would point their finger at me, stick their nose up at me, and whisper about me behind my back did no such thing. And I was pleasantly surprised.

After a few weeks of being a spectator, I walked into bible

study, once again dressed in my work uniform. My eyes were red and droopy from the weed I had smoked in the parking lot prior to entering church. About halfway through the bible lesson, Pastor Hearn stopped teaching. He looked at me in front of everyone and said, "Young lady!"

*Oh no, he's about to call me out.*

"The Lord is speaking to me about you."

*Oh man, I knew this was too good to be true. He's about to call me out in front of all these people and tell them that I'm high.*

He confidently said, "The Lord is telling me that you are going to lead our youth department."

*Wait? What? Who? Me? Umm...* All of those one-word questions zipped through my brain, and I turned around to look behind me, because surely the pastor was talking to someone other than me. He had to have been referring to someone else. I pointed to my heart with my index finger then softly said out loud, "Me?"

"Yes, you! The Lord is telling me that you're going to lead our youth department."

"Umm, amen?" That's all I said. That's all I could say.

I was high. I was a baby Christian. I still cussed. I still smoked a pack of cigarettes every day. I didn't know any bible verses by heart except for John 3:16. How in the world was God saying that He wanted me to lead a youth department? I didn't understand it. It made no sense to me.

It didn't have to. I knew that Pastor Hearn was being serious. But more than that, I knew that *the Lord* was being serious.

One Saturday morning about a month later, I stood before the church. I vulnerably shared my full testimony and assumed the position of Youth Director. There were moments I could hardly see the podium to read my notes through the tears in my eyes. I choked out my words in an attempt to explain my past and how God had encountered me that day in the hospital. Everything happened so fast, but God was moving, so I set my heart to run at His pace. He was just getting started.

The true presence of God was at New Start Ministry, and for the next seven years, I was there as often as I could be. Prayer meeting? I'm there. Bible study? I'm there. Sunday school? I'm there. Need help opening the church? You got it. Need help cleaning the bathrooms? You got it. Someone needs a ride? You got it. I was the first one there and among the last to leave, week in and week out. I was like a sponge—so hungry, zealous, and eager to absorb truth in every way. They taught me how to tarry and travail in prayer. They taught me about the gifts of the Holy Spirit and praying in tongues. They taught me how to serve others above myself and how to submit to authority.

But above all, they taught me how to love God, His Word, and His people. I wanted to just dwell in this place, with these people, forever. It was unlike anything I had ever known. The Lord had given me more than a new start.

He'd given me a new life.

# CHAPTER 18
# @MIRIAH_BORNAGAIN

*Where the mind goes, the body follows.*

here is an internal war in every born-again believer where the flesh and the Spirit are in conflict with each other. *"The flesh desires what is contrary to the Spirit, and the Spirit desires what is contrary to the flesh"* (Galatians 5:17). Sometimes that war can feel like a losing battle, but it's not supposed to.

When I was in the world, my whole being cried out to commit sins that felt good to my flesh. I never thought about how to please God or how to give Him glory. I never considered what it meant to pursue purity or to live free from sin. When I was living in sin, I could care less about these things. But once God gave me a new heart and a new spirit, His Holy Spirit, these things seemed to be all I could think about.

My life had meaning now, and I was motivated to pursue God's kingdom and God's ways. Even when my flesh tried to rear its ugly head, or my imagination tried to bring up old fantasies, or my brain tried to open lost files in an attempt to trigger old memories and mindsets, I clung to the truth that God has given us victory over our flesh through Jesus. Left to ourselves, our flesh will always choose sin. But thankfully, we are not left to ourselves.

The key to winning this internal war is to focus our mind on the Holy Spirit, the Spirit of Truth. He is present, dwelling within us, helping us every step of the way. When we choose to renew our mind with biblical truth, we begin to walk in life-giving freedom with God. We're free to pursue the spiritual realities of who we really are in Jesus, without being weighed down by sin or any obligation to our flesh. Our renewed mind is empowered to say yes to God's ways and God's truth. As we continue to learn and know the One who created us, we become more and more like Him.

My spirit had been made new when I repented on that bathroom floor, but my soul, (my mind, will, and emotions) still needed to follow suit. In order to combat this, Galatians 5:16 would have to become my reality. *"So I say, walk by the Spirit, and you will not gratify the desires of the flesh."* I was going to have to learn what it meant to "walk by the Spirit," or I would return again and again to gratify the desires of my flesh.

The Holy Spirit convicted my heart when I would cuss, lie, smoke, or do anything bad. It was like my mind had awoken to the fact that I wasn't just committing a bad action, but I was actually sinning directly against a loving God. And in the midst of sinning, I was hurting His heart, because He died to set me free from sin. And hurting His heart hurt my heart. So, with the help of the Holy Spirit, I said "yes" to the pruning and to the process of sanctification.

We talked earlier about how our bodies have dopamine receptors that trigger a "feel good" hormone anytime we do something pleasurable. I had to renew my mind to what pleasure actually is. The songs, books, movies, places, people, and things from my previous life didn't bring as much pleasure as they used to. I was no longer able to sin freely without remorse.

Deep down in my inner parts, I no longer wanted to do those things, but in my mind those things were all I had known for so long. Now keenly aware of my sin, it bothered me. I felt like I was a million-layer onion with dirty, scaly outer skins, and God was the Master Chef wanting to get down to those fleshy, inner skins, dealing with me layer by layer.

The Lord had given me a clean slate in the Spirit, but there were some things that I needed to take responsibility for in the natural.

I said earlier that God found me in the pit of hell, but He didn't leave me there. It's true. When the Holy Spirit came to live inside of me, He began to form the life of Christ in me. Ever so intentionally, God put His finger on the things in my life that had to go. He gently began to peel back the layers of my heart and strip them off one by one. With each new layer that the Holy Spirit peeled back, I felt Him inviting me deeper and deeper into His love and freedom. A tender heart and a sensitive conscience now replaced my hard heart and numb conscience.

In the weeks and months that followed, I stopped smoking weed and threw away every bit of drug paraphernalia that I had. I stopped watching pornography and masturbating, and if I tried to go back to look at it, I would feel sick to my stomach with disgust. I stopped using cuss words and listening to music and movies that had cuss words in them. Hearing or saying such words made my insides cringe. I flushed all my prescription anxiety pills down the toilet and never looked back. I got fired from my job at the breastaurant, and I stopped answering the phone for the pimps who used to pay for my body.

Surprisingly to me, cigarettes were the last and hardest thing for me to lay on the altar. Everything else had happened so fast, but the process of quitting cigarettes ultimately took a year before I finally quit for real. I tried to quit cold turkey three different times before I finally tired of sneaking around as a closet cigarette smoker. God used 1 Corinthians 6:19-20 to help me quit. "*Do you not know that your bodies are temples of the Holy*

*Spirit, who is in you, whom you have received from God? You are not your own; you were bought at a price. Therefore honor God with your bodies.*" Every time I craved a cigarette, I would quote that verse and envision the smoke filling my temple, filling my lungs, and choking out the Holy Spirit, who now lived in me. I didn't want to choke out God in me. I wanted to be free from anything that would contaminate me in any way.

The born-again conscience is tender and sensitive to the conviction of the Holy Spirit. The Bible calls this feeling *godly sorrow* or *godly grief*. It's when you actually feel bad for doing something wrong, and that sorrow leads you to repent. That sorrow will lead you to turn and run and not commit that sin again. That sorrow will lead you right to the feet of Jesus in full dependence on Him.

Countless times during the first couple of years of my walk with God, someone's name from middle or high school would pop into my head, and I instantly felt compelled to reach out to them and apologize for how I had wronged them. The Holy Spirit continually extended this invitation to die to myself and go deeper in Jesus. He steadily whispered, "Ask for forgiveness from this person. Forgive that person. Renounce and repent of every ungodly, sexual association that you can recall. Make right every wrong that you possibly can."

About a year after the guys who killed Amber and Chris had been locked away, God put it on my heart to write each of them a letter. I put it off for years because honestly, I didn't want to write them a letter. They deserved to be in prison for life. They deserved to feel guilty for what they did. They deserved every bit of righteous anger that I felt toward them. But every time I would remember Amber, I would remember these men who took her life. And every time I would remember these men who took her life, I would remember the men who took Jesus' life. And I would remember that even while they were brutally and viciously murdering Jesus, He extended forgiveness to them. He prayed, *"Father, forgive them, for they do not know what they are doing"* (Luke 23:34).

God called me to forgive these men. It wasn't enough for me to just confess out loud in the privacy of my home, "Lord, I forgive [their names]," many times over until it became my reality. God wanted me to extend that forgiveness to each of these men in a real and tangible way.

So, by the strength of God, I made the choice to release these hostages from the prison of my heart, and I hand wrote three individual letters that were pages upon pages long. I figured they have nothing but time, so I might as well bare my whole soul to them, as well as preach the Gospel. I made them remember Amber and what an amazing human she was. I painted them a picture of the beautiful life that they took into their own hands. I told them how much she was missed and what they stole, not only from her, but from her family and friends that she left behind.

Then, I cried as I wrote, *"...but, I forgive you."* I can still see the blue pen in my hand and the ink on the looseleaf paper as I tried my best to put into words that I forgave them, even if they weren't sorry. Then, I shared the beautiful story of God's deep love and how He, too, forgives them. I told them that it's only because of His love that I was able to write that letter in the first place. I told them of how God forgives even the murderers and how He died for the worst of the worst. He died for every sin, including theirs. And that if they would just turn to Him, He would forgive them and give them a brand-new life.

They're all still in prison today. I only ever heard back from one of those three men, thanking me for my letter. But I didn't care about hearing back from them. I only cared that they heard from me and that they heard about Jesus and the forgiveness that He extends to all.

Now, I wasn't perfect. There were times when I would look in the rearview mirror. There were moments when I would give into my flesh. But when I did, I experienced remorse. I'd feel gross. I'd feel sorry for my actions. I could no longer live peace-fully in that place. I could no longer sin undisturbed. God stripped me down bare, and I gladly let Him, even though it hurt sometimes.

The Holy Spirit in us gives us the power to deny our flesh. The Holy Spirit in us gives us the power to say, "No flesh, I will not call that boy. I will not smoke that blunt. I will not click on that website. I will not watch that movie." Romans 13:14 says not to even think about ways to give the flesh what it wants. Being fully immersed in Jesus means not wasting even a moment's thought on our former identity to awaken its old, selfish desires. In other words, when these old thoughts, desires, habits, or behaviors come knocking on the door of our new, born-again life, we should give no thought to how to satisfy them. Instead, we take those thoughts captive and proclaim, "I am not that person anymore. I don't do those things anymore. Thank You, Jesus, that I don't have to give in to temptation and sin." The mindset controlled by the Spirit truly finds life and peace.

There is something about the simplicity and the purity of the fire upon the life of a newly born-again Christian. Since I was no longer living for the world, my spiritual vision had changed completely. So much so that it almost felt like I could see things brighter with my natural, physical eyes. Colors were more vibrant. Life was livelier. With everything in me, I leaned into the freedom and joy that came with being born again.

I changed my Instagram name from @Miriajuana (marijuana) to @Miriah_BornAgain. Twelve years later, my personal Insta-gram name is still @Miriah_BornAgain. I can't bring myself to change it, because for me it holds so much weight. To some people it may only be a social media name tag, but the last time I changed that name, my entire life, existence, and person changed with it.

I never would have imagined that I would be one of "those Christians." You know, the kind that actually enjoy living their lives for Jesus. I never knew that living for Him could be so invigorating and fun. Sometimes, other people—even other Christians— tell me, "It doesn't take all that," or "You're holier than thou," or "You're doing too much." If anyone ever tells you that, just take all those statements with a grain of salt and keep your eyes fixed on Jesus. Because the thing is, not everyone will understand what the Lord has delivered you from. Not everyone will understand what He has brought you through. Not everyone will understand how He saved your literal life from the flames of hell. And not everyone will be happy for you in your born-again life. They won't all support you or agree with your born-again life—even family and close friends. And that is okay.

Those people weren't there when I was smoking crystal meth from a light bulb. They weren't there when I was cutting myself and burning my wrists and thighs with a lighter. When I was prostituting my body for money. When I was glued to my laptop and cell phone, addicted to pornography. They weren't there when I was heartbroken, listening to R&B love songs, crying myself to sleep. They weren't there when I was sleeping on a cold, metal jail cot or when I was crushing up pills and snorting them with a dollar bill in a bathroom stall. They weren't there when I was being used and abused by my so-called boyfriends. And when I took a bunch of pills, intending to end my own life, they weren't there.

Same for you. Those same people who tell you that "you've changed" or "you're doing too much" don't fully understand the magnitude of what God has done in your life. And that's perfectly okay. Keep doing too much and do even more! Go hard after Jesus through every critical word and past every judgmental eye. It actually does take all that, and if people only knew what He's brought you out of, maybe then they would understand your devotion and praise to Him.

But maybe not. And that's okay too. We aren't trying to win the approval of people, but of God. If pleasing people was our goal, we wouldn't be Christ's servants.

# CHAPTER 19

# HUNGER AND THIRST FOR RIGHTEOUSNESS

*True hunger can make us desperate, and humble desperation*
*is a magnet to the Holy Spirit.*

Y ou know that old saying, "A closed mouth don't get fed?" My mouth was wide open, and I was hungry for the Lord. As I began to read the Bible, I became obsessed with it. Tons of Scriptures on notecards and sticky notes covered my bedroom wall. I took my Bible with me everywhere I went. I just wanted to read it, to understand it. Reading His Word made me feel close to God. Reading it revealed who God was to me and who I was to Him. I was finally in a love relationship with the Person that I had been searching for my entire life. True Love had found me, and His name was Jesus.

As this new-found, deep love consumed me, the gift of evangelism was awakened in my life. I wanted everyone that I met to come to know this love, this Jesus. Even still!

But as we begin to operate in the gifting upon our lives, God also wants to make sure that we are rooted in the truth of His Word. Why? Because some of God's kids will love the gift more than the gift giver. And God doesn't want that for us. He loves us deeply. Above all, He wants us to know and intimately experience His precious love. He wants His precious love to be the motivator behind every action of our new, born-again life. And it should be from this place of revelation of His love that we live and burn for Him.

Revelation of His burning, passionate, precious love for us is not only all-consuming, but empowering. His love empowers us to touch the world around us. It empowers us to live holy and to love unconditionally. We don't have to work it up. We don't have to conjure it up. We just let Him love us. We receive His love by faith and believe that He died specifically for *us* on that cross. When we believe that, read it in the Bible, and renew our mind to accept it, then we will walk in freedom. We will walk in purpose. We will walk in joy and peace. We will walk burning, set ablaze by Love Himself.

I once heard someone say, "In the kingdom of God, things are a bit backward sometimes. In the natural world, the more you eat, the fuller you get. But in God's kingdom, the more you eat, the hungrier you get." How blessed we are when we crave and hunger for His righteousness. When we hunger for the person of Jesus and to live holy. Hunger for heaven on earth can be a literal driving force behind a surrendered life. Hunger can be wind in our sails, because when we're hungry, there's little that we wouldn't do to get food. Thankfully, He satisfies completely.

God values His Word, and time spent in it is never wasted. One year after being saved, I realized that I needed help understanding the Bible more. I was hungry for more than the magnifying glass that I had been using on my own, so I applied to go to a local discipleship school called The Evangelical Institute of Biblical Training (further referenced as EIBT). I thought they may reject my application to the school, because they asked some pretty in-depth questions. And me being me, I disclosed the full truth and nothing but the truth about my past. To my surprise, they called me back and told me that I had been accepted into the school.

Looking back, that was the most precious time during my early Christian walk. That program set the foundation of my life in the Word of God. For the next three years, I got to spend almost every day intentionally studying the Word of God. I learned the importance of the Bible and making it a habit to spend time reading it every day. We started every day with prayer, every class with prayer. Even volleyball games and kitchen and cleaning duties began with prayer. They trained us to intentionally invite the Lord into every moment and every action.

During my time at EIBT, I was an off-campus student, living with my mom in a one-bedroom apartment in the hood. I commuted to school every morning, stayed there all day for classes, and then went to work at 2PM. Back when I had lost my job at the breastaurant a year prior, my pastor was able to help me get a job with the Greenville County School district as a custodian. I got paid to clean throw up off of colorful ABC rugs and to clean poop that had been finger painted onto bathroom walls. Hey, there's a season for everything, right?

The Holy Spirit was cultivating excellence and integrity in me, something I really didn't care much about before I gave my life to Jesus. Most of the day I worked alone, so I'd put my head-phones in while I cleaned the elementary school classrooms and offices. Cleaning toilets, sweeping floors, mopping, taking out trash, dusting, wiping down desks—all minuscule tasks to the human eye. But to God, it was a training ground, a test of integrity and work ethic. I was learning how to be on time, how to be faithful, and how to not cut corners.

I was learning to work as unto the Lord, because even when no one else is watching, He is. Nothing goes unseen by His eye. If I saw a cobweb in the corner, I couldn't act as if I didn't see it. If I saw a piece of paper under a desk, I couldn't act as if I didn't see it. God is into the details. He wants us to do things the right way, even when no one else will ever know if we did them the wrong way. He really means it when He says in Colossians 3:23, *"Whatever you do, work at it with all your heart, as working for the Lord, not for human masters."*

So-and-so wasn't my boss; Jesus was my Boss. I learned to work with excellence, not because I feared losing my job, but because I wanted to please God. I wanted to glorify Him. I wanted Him to be seen in and through me in everything. So, if I was going to clean toilets, I was going to clean them well. Don't get me wrong, there were still times when I acted up on the job. There were times when I would hide and take naps in my custodial closet, times when I didn't mop behind a bookshelf, and times when I left that cobweb right where it was hanging. I didn't cross every *T* and dot every *I* perfectly, but the conviction was there. Every single time, I heard His still-small voice nudge me to go back and right my wrong.

It was humbling, for sure, but I really believe that anything that humbles us helps us. It's not about being the perfect employee or even the perfect Christian. It's about the character of Christ being formed in us. And everything in life—*everything* —is an opportunity for that forming to take place. If we allow it.

In my spare time, I worked with the youth, shared the gospel on the streets of downtown, and chased every glorious meeting or prayer gathering in the upstate that I could find. I would drive Ursula, my ol' faithful, black VW Jetta, from Greenville to Clemson to Greenwood to all over, attending twenty-four-hour prayer and worship events. I even drove all the way to Orlando, Florida by myself one time, for the Jesus Image conference. My life was and is consumed by Him, and I continue yearning to be in His presence and surrounded by people who love Him.

I led the youth group from this place of zeal, hunger, and sensitivity.

It was here that I would learn how to be a faithful steward with little or with much. Youth group was like a revolving door. There were seasons of busyness with fifteen-plus kids and seasons where one kid would show up. I remember a few times when no one showed up. Of course, I was disappointed, but honestly it wasn't too big of a problem. I would just go to the prayer room, pour my heart out to Jesus, lock up the church, and drive home in my little black Jetta. How many showed up each week made no difference to me; I would be there. Faithfully committed to what Jesus had called me to. Why? Because over the course of the next seven years, I would see many of them give their lives to Jesus.

I loved being with those young people. Whatever God was teaching and showing me, that's what I taught and showed them. The first message I ever taught them was on Ephesians 6:10-19, The Armor of God. We talked about how every Christian faces spiritual battles against unseen demonic forces, but God has given us the protection and the weapons that we need in order to fight. I brought six different props and let the youth hold and try on each piece of their spiritual armor. The belt of truth, breastplate of righteousness, shoes of peace, shield of faith, helmet of salvation, and sword of the spirit. We had a good time studying that passage.

But my story doesn't end with leading youth group. God really does satisfy the thirsty and fill the hungry with good things (See Psalm 107:9). For the first time in my life, I was truly happy. I was content. I was alive.

Full speed ahead, I ran forward in my new life in Christ. I didn't want to go backward, and I had no intention of doing so, but there was one major area of my life that I had yet to fully surrender to Jesus. And I ran headfirst into the trap that was set for me around the coming corner. A trap that I had willingly submitted myself to in times past, one that was all too familiar to me. Except it was a little different this time, because this trap was wrapped up pretty, with a big, red Jesus bow on top ...

# CHAPTER 20

# SLEEPING WITH THE STREET PREACHER

When it comes to red flags, we don't need ten before we finally yield. Just one red flag is enough.

very much still wanted to be in a physical relationship, to find "my person." I very much wanted to be married. But the guys who I was once attracted to didn't cut it anymore. Everything had been made new—even my desires for the type of man that I wanted. Now, I wanted a godly man. I wanted someone who could lead me, provide for me, make me feel secure, make me feel confident, and who would love me for me. I had been cheated on so many times that, ultimately, I wanted a man who would choose me and only me.

It's crazy, because old Miriah, now dead Miriah, would have simply settled for a man who didn't cuss at her. A man who didn't put his hands on her and didn't want to use her for sex. A man who wasn't embarrassed to call her his. But *new* Miriah has standards. New Miriah has self-respect. New Miriah knows that I am loved by Jesus. New Miriah knows that I'm accepted. New

Miriah knows that I'm seen. New Miriah knows her worth. Or so I thought.

From day one of giving my life to Him, I told the Lord, "I will live pure."

No more pornography. No more masturbation. No more sexting. No more sending nude pictures. No more chat rooms, one-night stands, or booty calls. No more lusting after men and women. "No more, Lord!" I even went as far as no more watching movies with sex scenes in them or listening to any secular music, because it's all so laced with sexual perversion.

I didn't even want to see people through the lenses of my natural eyes anymore. I didn't want to look at anyone according to the flesh (See 2 Corinthians 5:16). Every single human is a soul, wrapped in flesh and clothed in linen. God looks at the heart and not the outward appearance, and so that is what I wanted to do too. I wanted to only see people as souls, as God's creations.

And while my desires for a godly man were good, the Lord began to show me that I wasn't as secure in His love as I thought I was. He began to show me that I still needed to renew my mind around how valuable I actually was. I still needed to renew my mind around my worth.

Sure, I'd come a mighty long way. After all, I was no longer prostituting my body. I was no longer having sex. I was no longer watching porn. But because God looks at the heart, He saw that mine was not fully, one hundred percent at rest in His Love. What I mean by this is that I still wanted to be in a relationship so badly that instead of chasing ungodly men like I used to do, I just switched up the type, and I began to chase godly men. This was a problem, because God never wanted me to chase anything or anyone other than Him.

Chase is a game played by kids where one kid runs after another kid that is trying to get away. Once caught, the kid says, "Got you!" The chaser exudes all of his strength and energy, but the chase-ee doesn't actually want to get caught. It's a fun and innocent game meant for kids, *not meant for hearts*. The Lord wanted me to realize that my heart wasn't a game to Him. My heart wasn't a joke to Him. My body wasn't a tool or a toy to Him. As His daughter, I wasn't something to be played with. I didn't know that I didn't have to go on a wild goose chase trying to figure out who my husband would be. But when you're in the thick of it, that is easier said than done.

I swore that "God told me so-and-so was my husband" multiple times. I wasted time on three different "counterfeits" before the man I was actually supposed to be with found me. Two of them were genuinely good, godly men, just not the men for me. But that third one, honey, 2 Corinthians 11:14, through and through. That verse says, *"Satan himself masquerades [or disguises] as an angel of light."*

I first saw him preaching the gospel on the street corners of downtown Greenville in November of 2015. I had to do a double take, because I thought I had seen a literal angel of light. I thought I had seen Michael, my ex, who died in that motorcycle accident in 2013. Street preacher looked exactly like him. He was tall and had long dark hair. What really triggered me was that he was Asian. Street preacher reminded me so much of Michael that I almost cried just looking at him. Street Preacher came packaged up just how I needed him to, with a big, red bow on top— disguised as an angel of light.

It only took about a month of knowing him before I found myself spending the night at his house and, ultimately, sleeping with him. And not the kind of sleeping you do with your eyes closed.

You play the devil's games, you win the devil's prizes. I had consecrated my life and pursued purity with Jesus for three years straight. I was leading a youth group and still attending bible school when I willingly allowed myself to be deceived back into sexual sin. Immediately after it happened, I cried and cried with regret. Yet, I didn't end the relationship, nor did I leave him. I stayed with him.

I consistently ignored my friends, who kept telling me that he was no good for me. I also ignored my pastors, who rightly discerned that Street Preacher was pulling me away from the Lord. They had met him in person, and they saw what I couldn't see. When I confessed to my pastors that Street Preacher and I had slept together, they removed me from my post as youth director. They encouraged me to repent. They told me to break it off with him. But I didn't listen to them. I dismissed the counsel of those closest to me and ignored red flag after red flag.

I followed my own desires, and I followed Street Preacher right into the bedroom. I was so deceived and blinded by my desire to be in a relationship that I made excuses for my sin. Street Preacher would say things like, "I'm gonna marry you," or "You're my wife, so what we're doing is totally fine." He even used the Bible to try to justify why what we were doing was okay, perverting the Scriptures, twisting them into half-truths and false teachings. And I went right along with him, blinded by my desire to love and be loved.

What's even more disgusting is that every time we would go out in public, we would share the Gospel with others. We saw many get touched by Jesus and even led a handful of people to surrender their lives to Jesus. We were doing the Lord's work. People were getting saved. *Surely* he was the one God had for me, right? Wrong. So, *so* wrong. And deep down, I knew it was wrong, but I continued in it anyway. I continued to sin and say sorry. And sin and say sorry. And sin and say sorry.

I really did feel bad for what I was doing, but the deception was strong, and instead of fighting my flesh, I gave in to it. As I fed my flesh like a pet, it continued to grow stronger and stronger. I wasn't truly happy, but I thought that maybe, *just maybe*, Street Preacher would be my husband. Even though, deep down, I knew that he wouldn't. It was a mess. The entire situation was a whole, hot mess.

One night, while Street Preacher was in the shower, I felt so disgusting and full of shame just for being in his house that I fell to my knees on his kitchen floor and hid myself behind a small rolling cart, as if to tuck myself away from the world. I wanted to curl up into a ball and hide forever. Shame covered me like a blanket. I looked toward heaven, and I wept. Once again, I told the Lord I was sorry for being with this man, sorry for putting myself back into the very cesspool of sin that He had pulled me out of years ago.

As I sat there, quietly weeping, I heard the Lord speak to my heart. "You can stay here. You can stay here with him, and you can choose to be with him, and this will be your life. This will be your posture every single night. You will live a life of sadness and weeping, crying on your knees every night."

I didn't want that. But it seemed like I was in so deep now that I didn't even know how to get out. I wanted to leave him, but I didn't want to leave him. It all appeared innocent and even godly at first. Satan had pulled me in and tangled me in his web. Street Preacher was dressed in sheep's clothing as an angel of light, but inwardly he was a dangerous wolf, an angel of darkness. A messenger of Satan sent to tempt me, to steal from me, to kill me, and ultimately to destroy me.

Less than two months. That's all it took for me to go from burning, on fire, happy, and healthy to lukewarm, miserable, tainted, and broken. And you wanna know something crazy? I wasn't even the one to end the relationship. He was. One random day shortly after Christmas, he broke things off and told me he wanted to try to work things out with his wife! *Wait? Wife?* I was dumbfounded. He had told me they were divorced, but it turns out they were only separated and had been married all along. *Lord, have mercy on me!*

He ended things, and we never spoke or saw each other again. I was left broken, discarded, rejected, and humiliated, like I had been so many times before. And because I had given sin an open door in my life, I had once again coasted effortlessly on my bike of sin down to the bottom of the hill. But it wasn't until a few weeks later, when I got off the bike and turned around to look back at the hill, that I realized how far I had actually fallen. And that uphill climb was daunting.

My experience with Street Preacher taught me that even the very elect can be deceived (See Matthew 24:24). I had cracked the door to the devil, and he'd swung that thing wide open and entered with full force. I needed deliverance after my encounters with Street Preacher. I was beyond heartbroken and disappointed in myself.

David wrote in Psalm 32:1-5, "*Blessed is the one whose transgressions are forgiven, whose sins are covered. Blessed is the one whose sin the LORD does not count against them and in whose spirit is no deceit. When I kept silent, my bones wasted away through my groaning all day long. For day and night your hand was heavy on me; my strength was sapped as in the heat of summer. Then I acknowledged my sin to you and did not cover up my iniquity. I said, 'I will confess my transgressions to the LORD.' And you forgave the guilt of my sin.*"

I laid in the back room of my church, New Start Ministry, weeping from the deepest places of my being, as Sister Hearn (my pastor's wife) and another sister in Christ prayed over me. They commanded the demons that I had opened myself up to, to leave my life in Jesus name. They released healing words over me, and they lovingly held me as I laid there.

When we backslide—or even stumble—the lies of the devil sweep in and try to hold us hostage in that place of regret, shame, and guilt. We must refuse to remain hostage to anything demonic, be it sin or be it shame. Trust me and believe when I say that the devil was shooting fiery darts of accusation and condemnation at me daily. "You haven't changed!" "You're the same old girl!" "You're worthless!" "No one is ever going to really love you!" "You really screwed up this time, you might as well go back to how you used to live!"

That liar! I had changed. I wasn't the same old girl. For months, I had to remind myself of Romans 8:1, that "*there is now no condemnation for those that are in Christ Jesus.*" We may fall, but we must repent and rise again. Because when we get up again, when we keep moving forward, when we turn the corner, we will be amazed at what the Lord has prepared for us and how the Lord redeems all we've done. The enemy was going to regret the trap that he had set for me; Jesus would make sure of it.

You see, God didn't just save me that one time on August 13, 2013. He's a good and patient Father. He has faithfully and continually saved me each time I've stumbled, fallen, and even ran headfirst back into sin. Jesus thought I was worthy enough to God that He gave His life for me. Jesus loves me like crazy. And yeah, I did screw up big time, but God didn't want me to go back to the way that I used to live; He wanted me to come back to Him.

Even though once I repented, the Lord instantly forgave me and saw me no differently in His sight, it took months for me to mentally and emotionally recover and to see myself that way again. Renewing my mind was an uphill trek. I purposed in my heart and begged the Holy Spirit to never let me step foot outside of His will in that way, ever again. Then, I took the necessary time to heal.

I wasn't allowed to minister at church. Not because I was being punished, but because I needed to prove to myself and to my community that I could be trusted again. My disobedience hadn't affected only myself. When a leader falls, those connected to that leader are affected too. I watched the flame of the youth group that I once led begin to dwindle. After about six months of sitting down and healing, I was restored to my position as youth director, and Psalm 119:9 became the theme of my heart and of our youth group. *"How can a young person stay on the path of purity? By living according to Your word."*

How can a young person (or any person) stay pure? How can we remain in the love of Jesus after many years of being born again? It's by His grace alone that we are saved and by His grace alone that we can live holy. We must live according to the Word of God. Be quick to repent and run from anything that causes us to stumble. Be quick to acknowledge that we need Him. Continuously receive His grace by faith. We don't have time to stay wallowing in condemnation or shame. Get up! The Lord is so rich in mercy, and He delights in showing it.

I didn't know that I was going to include my "Street Preacher" story in this book, but I felt the Lord asking me to share it with you. I don't want this book to be a story of a bad girl who became a good girl and lived happily ever after. I think it's important to be honest and say that I have wrestled through many struggles, even after coming to the Lord. I haven't walked perfectly before Him. I've made many, many mistakes. Proverbs 24:16 says, *"for though the righteous fall seven times, they rise again."*

I don't want to make excuses for the flesh or for sin. But I want to encourage you that if you stumble, if you fall, if you backslide, you can and should repent and rise again. His grace was enough to save you in the beginning, and it's enough to save you even now. I want you to know that it doesn't matter what horrible places you've been to or what disgusting things you've done. If you turn to Jesus in the midst of your mess, He will meet you where you are, and He won't leave you where He finds you.

This book is a story about a God who has a plan for your life. A God who can save anyone, no matter where you've been or what you've done. This is a story about a God who takes broken hearts and makes them whole again. Who finds the lost and brings the dead to life. Who restores, redeems, and renews us over and over and over again. It's a story about a God who takes what was designed to destroy us and uses it for His glory.

You are beautiful. You are valuable. You are loved. You are precious. You are special. You are accepted in Him. God is at work in you, giving you the desire and the power to do what pleases Him. You can do what pleases Him, and that should always be your pursuit.

Come back to Him if you need to! Run back with all that is within you. You may not be sleeping with a street preacher like I was, but I challenge you to examine your life and repent of any areas of sin that come to your mind. Whether big or small, you can begin afresh right now. Your sin does not define you. Don't behold your sin. Behold Jesus. And He will make you new again and again and again.

If that is you today, I encourage you to pray to the Lord. Let Him be your hiding place again. He will protect you from trouble, and He will surround you with songs of deliverance. He wants to instruct you and teach you in the way you should go. Allow Him to counsel you with His loving eye on you.

# CHAPTER 21
# IN THE WAITING SEASON

*"At the right time, I, the Lord, will make it happen."*
Isaiah 60:22 (NLT)

I have come to learn that just as we go through seasons in the world—spring, summer, fall, and winter—we go through seasons in the spirit realm as well. Spiritual seasons are not perfectly marked by specific dates on a calendar, and the transition from one season to the next isn't always smooth and seamless. But when you *"Trust in the Lord with all your heart and lean not on your own understanding,"* as it says in Proverbs 3:5, there is a straight path that He will lead you on, season by season.

Every season is carefully structured with intention. Purpose and joy can be found in both the valley seasons and the mountaintop seasons. Each contains an opportunity for the character of Christ to be formed in us and for the fire of God to burn in us. We can be sure that His desire is not for us to be stuck, trapped, or paralyzed. His desire is never for us to stay in the wilderness. He truly desires for us to go from glory to glory.

That's where I'm at and what I'm learning to do. I could share many practical stories from those first few years of being born again. The stripping, the exposing, the refining, the purifying, the sanctifying, the repenting, the forgiving, the confessing, the growing, the stretching, the learning, the maturing. But the truth is, I'm still in it, even after twelve years of knowing Jesus. I'm ever learning that on my darkest, most lonely wilderness night, Jesus is just as near to me as He is on my brightest, most glorious morning.

All of the shame, stress, and heartache that came with Street Preacher and my bad decisions caused me to wanna run into the arms of Jesus all the more. I found myself at Jesus' feet, even more desperate for Him. This wilderness season of backsliding had broken me. But it also humbled me. And whatever humbles us has the potential to help us. If we let it. It's in this season that I realized I can truly do nothing apart from Him.

As I continued to look to Jesus, life slowly got back to normal. I did the things I did in the beginning of my life as a born-again Child of God. The joy and the fire of God returned, and my face radiated His light again. I sang in the shower again. With His help, I slowly rebuilt the bridges that I had burned with my leaders and closest friends. I had repented and returned to my First Love, my True Love, Jesus. And I was happy in that place.

But I really, really still desired to be married. I wanted a person, one person, *my* person who I could run after the Lord with, who I could laugh with, who I could cry with, who I could journey through life with until my dying breath.

I've always been a sucker for love. A hopeful romantic. Despite my heart getting broken many times over, I never became so jaded and bitter that I gave up on the desire to love and be loved by another. I've always believed each of us is born with that deep desire to know love. I don't think it's a wrong desire. I believe this desire is God-given. After all, isn't love what

God is really about? His great love for us? I also believe that it's God who gives that person to us. I believe that our spouse was preordained, our children were preordained. Our bloodline, our ministry, our entire life and every intricate detail of it is perfectly known by our good and perfect Father. The hard part is that God gives us these blessings on His timeline, not our own.

Enter the waiting season.

I find it super interesting that, in the Hebrew language, there are four different words for the word *wait*. When we see the word *wait* in the Hebrew scriptures, we find *qavah*, to hope or bind together; *yachal*, to wait with hope or expectation; *chakah*, to wait for a long time; and *chuwl*, to writhe, be in pain, or long anxiously. I dare to say that we will each experience at least one, if not all of these types of waiting as we journey through the different seasons of life.

Even when we don't understand, comprehend, or agree with how God might choose to go about things, we must remember that He is God, and we are not. He knows all; we know in part. He knows your story from beginning to end. All the days of your life have been written long before you were even born.

When we know the character of our Father, then we trust that He is always good. Which means that His timing and His plans are always good, and that understanding is a great comfort during times of waiting. Knowing God's heart toward me—that He loves me and has a good and perfect plan for me—is what ultimately kept me during the waiting.

I started off with that *qavah* sort of waiting. I found myself entwined with Jesus, bound to Him, eagerly waiting for Him to fulfill my heart's desire. I had a strong, deep-seated belief in God's faithfulness and sovereignty.

*Qavah* went hand in hand with *yachal*, because being entwined so closely to Jesus gave me confidence and high expectations that God was going to send my husband. I rejoiced with my friends who entered into relationships, hopeful that I would be next. In ancient Hebrew culture, *yachal* waiting was not merely a passive activity, but it was an active expression of faith. I patiently waited and trusted God's timing.

But as the months passed by and time stretched on, I grew more and more eager to meet my God-given husband. When it seemed like everyone around me was receiving their promise except for me, *qavah/yachal* gave way to *chakah* and my patience began to be tested. I was still expectant, still hopeful, but there was a shift from simply waiting to deeply longing.

In this longing, I had to fight against anxiety and impatience. Doubts crept in, and I questioned God's goodness, wondering if He was really going to come through for me. I was tempted to believe lies like: "God's plans for you are not good." "God has forgotten you." "Your husband will never come." "You're not wife material." "You should just settle for a lukewarm guy." And a bunch of other foolish lies.

When you're in the thick of that waiting, be it for a spouse, any other thing, or part of life, it can sometimes be hard to not lose hope. We sometimes grow weary, frustrated, or discouraged. The temptation can be to take matters that belong to God into our own hands. But what if these times of desperation are meant to be invitations into deeper depths of trust and surrender?

The Bible came to be a plumbline for my soul on the nights when I felt as though I wanted to give up. *Chaka* eventually gave way to *chuwl*, and it felt as though I had been waiting for a lifetime. I struggled to remain patient, living amidst a microwave, overnight delivery, DoorDash society. It wasn't easy.

When we are waiting on God to fulfill a promise or answer a prayer, sometimes it may feel as though we're writhing in pain like a woman in labor, longing anxiously for the birth of something really great. *Chuwl.* I know that God carefully structures every season with intentionality, often to stretch and grow and mature us in ways that immediacy never could. But that doesn't always feel good. In fact, there were nights when I wept until my stomach hurt and I groaned until I lost my voice. Days when the loneliness was almost unbearable, and the yearning could be physically felt.

Times where I had to make the choice to hold onto the truth that "God is good." Because holding onto the truth about God's goodness will keep us through the high and hard, as well as the low and easy seasons of waiting. The only way to wait in such a way is to be rooted in the truth of God's word.

The Bible is true, and there are thousands of promises that we can cling to as we wait. Lamentations 3:25 says, "*The LORD is good to those whose hope is in him, to the one who seeks him.*" Micah 7:7 says, "*But as for me, I watch in hope for the LORD, I wait for God my Savior; my God will hear me.*" Seeking and clinging to such promises will pick us up and carry us through the different seasons of life.

God's written Word is enough. Yet sometimes, God, being the good Father that He is, will send someone to speak a prophetic word over you. Spoken prophetic words that are truly from the Holy Spirit will always align with God's written word and will bear witness within your own spirit (See Romans 8:16).

We see in Luke 2:22-40 how all of Jerusalem had been waiting for the Messiah and the fulfillment of the prophetic words concerning Him. Throughout Scripture we also see that over the course of thousands of years, the Israelites were well acquainted with waiting. They experienced seasons of *qavah, yachal, chakah* and *chuwl* many times over.

But regardless of whether you are clinging to the spoken or the written words of God, you can be sure that His word will never return void. Even when it hurts, is uncomfortable, or takes decades, waiting on the Lord is never in vain. God is rarely early, but He is never late, and He is always right on time.

The seasons of life are constantly changing. In them, I, myself, am constantly changing. But Jesus and His Word forever remain the same. He is steadfast, so you and I can be too. He is that anchor that holds us in place when the winds of life are blowing. Yet He is the Wind itself that moves us along into each season at the proper time.

I prayed endlessly that my "proper time" would come soon. That my future husband would come soon. I was deeply longing for the birth of something really great, when the Lord spoke to me through a stranger.

# CHAPTER 22
# "HANDPICKED"

True love is friendship set on fire.

One Saturday morning, the women at our church decided to take a prayer walk, and I joined them. We went to one of the sisters' apartment complexes and walked around the entire complex as we prayed over our city and the people in it. Just as we were about to finish up, one sister suggested that we go into the leasing office and pray over it and over the employees there. When we walked in, to our surprise, we ran into a small group of women having a Bible study right there in the leasing office.

When we asked if we could join them, they welcomed us with joy, and we had a lovely time. At the end of the meeting, the woman leading it asked if she could pray over us. "Oh! Of course," we said. She went down the line, laid her hands on us one by one, and prayed specific, Spirit-filled prayers. It was like she had a direct line to God. She prophesied individual words of encouragement, things that only God would have known, and things that only God could have revealed to her.

Before she got to me, I took my iPhone out and clicked on the Voice Memos app, then clicked the little red recording button. I wanted to record what she was praying over us, because I knew that the words she spoke were from the Father's heart, and I didn't want to forget a single one.

Third in line, when my turn came to receive prayer, I held out my hands like a little kid about to receive a present. She gave me powerful word about being a worshiper of God and leading thousands of young people to the Lord. She said many other things that blew my mind, because again, only God could have revealed these things to her. It was awesome, and just when I thought that she was done speaking to me, she said one last thing, ending with these words:

"Oh! And I hear the Lord say He's got something special for you. *Handpicked*. I hear the Lord say, '*Handpicked*.' He has picked you a man, and this man is after God's heart. He is a man after God's own heart. As you wait, keep your hands busy in the Kingdom of God. Whatever you find for your hands to do, do it baby. It's a sustaining grace when you do the work of the Lord."

This happened in October of 2016, and those words kept me. Those words were roots to me. They were an anchor of hope for me during the waiting. I can't tell you how many times I went back and replayed that voice memo. I listened to it, I wrote it down in my journal, and I recited it to myself over and over in my season of waiting. "*Handpicked*," I would tell myself. "The Lord has *handpicked* a specific man for me."

Those words caused me to go even harder after God. I took those words to heart, and I kept myself busy with the things of God, even more so than I had done in times past. A man after God's heart wants a woman after God's heart. As I continued to pursue the heart of God, I trusted that my man would find me. The husband God had for me was going to find and pursue me, not the other way around.

Seven long months later, at the end of May 2017, I received a text message from one of my best friends that caught me completely by surprise. I still remember where I was and the utter shock that hit me when I read that text. I was out of town, visiting my sister Sydney in Savannah, Georgia. Around 11PM, I was laying on her couch, minding my own business, when my phone dinged.

It was a message from Joe Taverna—a long message, very calculated and very direct.

As I read it, my heart dropped. The gist of it said something along the lines of:

> I've been praying for months, asking God if I can pursue you. And He has given me permission to do that. I don't want to play games with you. I don't want to put your heart on a yo-yo. I want to date you. And I want you to know that if you say yes to dating me, that my intention is to marry you.

*Wait ... what did I just read?*

I couldn't reply. I was speechless. I had zero clue that he felt this way about me.

My first thought was, *No way! I can't date Joe. My friend has a crush on him.* Because of this, Joe had never even been on my husband radar. *Hello, girl code!* He being a marriage prospect for me was never a thought I'd entertained. Not only that, at the time, *I* had a crush on one of *Joe's* friends. So, when I received that text message, it caught me completely off guard.

The crazy thing is that my friend who had a crush on Joe ended up meeting the man who is now her husband one week after Joe texted me. And Joe's friend that I had a crush on got engaged to the woman who is now his wife around this same time. God had gone before me, and it felt like a divine setup that seemed too good to be true. Was this amazing man, who had been my friend for years, the "handpicked one?" Could it be that the one I had been waiting for had been right in front of my face all along?

My second thought was, *Joe is too good and too godly for me.* What a lie! Even after all that time waiting, these old thoughts and insecurities tried to rear their ugly heads in my life. This man basically just knocked on my front door and got down on one knee with a ring in his hand, and I was over there saying to myself, "He can't *really* be serious. He's too good and godly for me." I was tempted to believe the lie, that I wasn't good enough or godly enough for him. But the truth is I *was* and I *am.* And Joe saw that in me.

The person that God has chosen for you will see you through the lens of Jesus. They will love you for you. You won't have to pretend to be someone you're not for them to love you. You won't have to wonder if they truly love you. I don't know how else to explain it, except to say that when you know, you know. And when it's truly a God thing, you'll know. Promise.

So, what was my response to his text? I couldn't sleep that whole night. I stayed up praying, "God, what do I say to this?" I ended up texting him back around 7AM and said something like:

> Wow, that is so sweet of you, and honestly, that sounds really great, but I'm sorry, I can't date you. One of my friends likes you, and I can't do that to her.

He was so confused. I couldn't tell him who liked him. *Girl code.* But it didn't really matter to him anyway, because he would not take "no" for an answer. For the next week, he texted me flirty messages every day, asked to take me to lunch or dinner, and he even asked if we could just hang out like we used to.

When we were just friends, we could hang out for hours, just talking about Jesus and the Bible. We would go to Waffle House and sit and talk about the Lord until two and three o'clock in the morning. He was one of the few people that would sit with me and talk about the Bible for long periods of time without getting bored or irritated. Our friendship had been that way for years, but it was very platonic. We only ever did God stuff and talked about God stuff.

But now that the cat was out of the bag, there was no putting it back in. I couldn't just hang out with him and ignore the pink elephant in the room. I couldn't just look into those big, bright, amber eyes and see that precious smirk on his face in the same friendship light anymore. Love had been awakened by his text message, and I wrestled with how to move forward.

About a week after that message, I agreed to meet him at Panera Bread for dinner. But I made it clear, "This is *not* a date." I even wore leggings and a T-shirt in order to look like I hadn't put any effort into my appearance that day, making sure he knew this most definitely was *not* a date.

When I showed up at Panera, he paid for my food, and we sat at a table. Anyone who knows me knows that I love to eat, and I love to talk. I didn't touch my food that night. I could barely talk. Nervous, I had butterflies and felt like a little girl. I was giddy as I tried pretending like I wasn't interested in dating him, but there was no denying it. It all felt so pure and innocent. It felt right.

We stayed at Panera until they closed at 10PM. We weren't ready to leave each other yet, so he asked if I wanted to go to IHOP and have a cup of coffee for a little bit. Of course, I said yes. We got into his car and drove onto the highway.

All of a sudden, Joe says, "I want to hold your hand."

"Well then, do it," I blurted out, without thinking.

And he did. As soon as our fingers interlocked, the tangible presence of God filled his BMW.

A few minutes later, we pulled into the IHOP parking lot and parked the car. While instrumental worship music played, we continued holding hands. As what felt like bolts of electricity shot through our bodies, we both shook and twitched. The Holy Spirit had filled the car and met us with His presence in a very real way. It was electrifying, powerful, and unlike anything I had ever experienced. We sat there for at least an hour. Neither of us dared to say a word. What would we even say? We refused to disturb this holy moment. We soaked it in. We sank into it and rested there. We didn't fully understand what was happening, but we didn't need to. It was like God was communicating to us, "This is My stamp of approval. I am about this relationship. My Hand is upon this relationship." It was beautiful. It was Jesus.

We never went inside of IHOP. Joe drove me back to my car at Panera Bread, and on Cloud Nine, I left and drove to my house.

The following morning, June 10, 2017, we met up again and drove to a place called The Potters Place in Central, South Carolina. The Potters Place is a beautiful plot of land consecrated and set aside for people to come and spend alone time with God. We went to pray, read, and just worship the Lord. While there, Joe handed me a brown gift bag. In the bag were two bottles of these really great vitamins, an avocado, and a little index card. On the card he had written, *Will you be my girlfriend? Check 'yes,' 'no,' or 'maybe.'* After what we had experienced the night before, I knew that I knew that I knew he was God's handpicked promise that I had been waiting on.

The rest is history.

By August, just two short months later, we wanted to elope. Like we do with all major life decisions, we decided to pray and ask the Lord when we could get married. We prayed separately and both heard, "April." That felt like an eternity away for two young people who were burning with passion and ready to start their life together. Praise Jesus that He met us to wait with purity and keep ourselves until our wedding night.

I had the entire wedding planned out before Joe bought an engagement ring and proposed. Eight months later, on April 28, 2018, we said, "I do."

Cece Winans' "Alabaster Box" played in the background as I walked slowly to the altar in my vintage wedding dress, which my mom and I thrifted from Goodwill. Time seemed to stand still. My cheeks hurt from smiling, and my eyes glimmered with a joy brighter than the brightest star.

It was the second-best day of my life. Second only to August 13, 2013, the day that I gave my life to Jesus.

I waited my whole life to have someone look at me the way Joe does. A man who would love me for me, not for what I can do for him. A man who doesn't see me through the eyes of my past, but through the eyes of Jesus. A man after God's own heart.

God had slowly but surely dismantled the lies that I believed as a little girl. He'd uprooted those rotten seeds of Satan that started me down the path of death all those years ago.

First, He dismantled the lie that *true love doesn't exist*. The night He hugged me with His blanket of peace on the hospital floor, His love broke in and changed everything. But now, through Joe, God had dismantled the lie that *no one loves me*. It still brings tears to my eyes that Joe would choose me. More than that, God would choose me.

Stepping into marriage was stepping into a promise fulfilled, a love story written by God Himself. And in true God fashion, He had been working another miracle behind the scenes that I was totally unaware of. A miracle that went beyond the natural eye. A miracle of restoration. A testimony of His power to redeem what I thought had been lost forever.

# CHAPTER 23
# GOD RESTORED MY VIRGINITY

Miracles aren't just events; they are expressions of God's endless love and power, where the impossible becomes the undeniable.

B efore landing the plane in this book and bringing it to an end, I must share this last miraculous story, because it reiterates God's love, power, grace, mercy, forgiveness, and redemption. What God did next left me in complete awe.

I lost count of how many sexual partners I had before I gave my life to Jesus. Too many to count. But after I initially was born again in 2013, I made a purity vow to myself and to the Lord that I would not have sex again until I was married to my husband.

Sadly, I broke that vow when I met Street Preacher in 2015. I don't believe in living in regret, but I was disappointed in myself for breaking that first vow. I wanted to be able to tell my future husband, "I waited for you." I thought I had ruined the chance to be able to say that, but the Lord assured me that I had not.

The freedom that comes with surrendering your life to Jesus is hard to put into words. When you pray things like, "I don't want to live for myself anymore, I want to live for You now," He takes you seriously. And in living for Him, there is no shame. You no longer have to live under the cloud of what you did (or didn't do) last year—or even last night. Every morning, the sun rises to shine on you with a second chance to surrender again. Every day is an opportunity to say no to sin and yes to Him. An opportunity to seek His face, to read His word, and to come to know His heart. To give Him away to the world around you. To love and be loved. To live, unashamedly.

After things ended with Street Preacher, I made a second vow to the Lord. I determined that I would not give my body to another until after I walked down the aisle and said, "I do." I still had time to wait and to keep myself pure for my husband.

The Holy Spirit met me, and by His Spirit, I was able to successfully deny my flesh. When I walked down the aisle to meet Joe, I had been celibate for three years, and Joe had been celibate for four years. Only by God's grace!

But that's not where it ends. Listen to how faithful God is to forgive and to fully cleanse us of our sins whenever we confess and truly turn away from them.

The working definition of a *miracle* is a logic-defying event that cannot be explained by natural or scientific laws and is therefore considered to be the work of a divine, supernatural agency. Simply put, a miracle is a sign, a wonder, or a demonstration of the power and the greatness of God. Would you believe me if I told you that God performed a creative miracle in my body? What if I told you that God restored my virginity? God really does make all things new. I know it may sound crazy. It sounds logic-defying. It sounds impossible. But it's true. God actually restored my virginity.

I was listening to a podcast hosted by a man named Kris Vallaton called *Moral Revolution*. It's a podcast all about revolutionizing sex through a biblical lens. At the end of the podcast, Kris said that he was going to pray for anyone who had previously had sex and wanted to believe for God to supernaturally restore their virginity. He shared how he had prayed for women before and had seen God move in their lives. Those same women testified later how God had restored their virginity and even recreated their hymen.

I was mind-blown. I had never heard of or even thought of such a thing. But I wanted that! So, as I listened to him pray, I held out my hands and received that supernatural restoration in my own body, by faith. Obviously, I couldn't see anything happening within me, and I didn't feel anything either. I simply trusted that God saw me, God heard me, and that God wanted to do this for me. God is all about redeeming, restoring, and renewing the impossible. I thought to myself, *He is able. There is nothing too hard for Him. And if He did it for those other women, why wouldn't He do it for me?* I believed by faith that it was done.

Mind you, this was around 2015, before I even knew who my husband would be, before I even had a boyfriend. I simply believed, and I left it at that.

In a Jewish marriage covenant, the consummation is one of the most important steps. The Jewish culture values purity. They see consummation, the act of making your covenant complete through intercourse, as a huge and holy deal. In Deuteronomy 22:13-17, we see that when a married couple is intimate for the first time, blood gets on the bed sheet. When a woman has intercourse for the first time, her hymen is broken, causing her to bleed a bit. That bed sheet would then be kept by the parents of the bride as proof of her virginity.

To many scientists, the purpose of a woman's hymen is an eternal mystery. I believe that God created everything with intention, including creating women who have a hymen that can only be broken once in their lifetime as evidence of their purity. He could've given us a hymen for multiple reasons. But one of those reasons, I believe, is so that a woman can make a blood covenant with her husband. Blood covenants are considered the ultimate form of contract. We see the shedding of animal blood in God's covenants with Abraham and with Moses. We also see the shedding of Jesus' blood in God's New Testament covenant with us.

In our Western culture, the concept of saving ourselves for marriage, protecting that holy covenant with God and with our spouse, is somewhat of a foreign concept to us today, as it seems that we are drifting further and further away from valuing holiness and the sanctity of marriage. Everything is sexualized, and that sexualization has been normalized.

But in the eyes of Jesus, purity is still a requirement. Purity matters to Him, and it should matter to us too. If you want to walk closely with the Lord, if you want to see Him and know Him, then you must pursue consecration and holiness, because without it, you will never see Him (See Hebrews 12:14).

On April 29, 2018, the day after our wedding, Joe and I honeymooned to Sevierville, Tennessee for a whole week of heaven on earth. Once we got to our perfect, cozy cabin in the Smoky Mountains and were intimate for the first time, there was a bit of blood on the sheet. When I looked down and saw it, I wept. I remembered how I had prayed that the Lord would not only restore my virginity, but that He would specifically restore my hymen so that I would be able to make a blood covenant with my husband one day. Given my promiscuous past, there is no logical explanation for what happened that day, other than the fact that God performs miracles and there is nothing too hard for Him.

Why do I share this story with you? Because I pray that it builds your faith and encourages you that God can do it. Whatever *it* is. Whatever you are believing for, God can do it. No matter how bad you think you may have messed things up, God can restore it. No matter how big of a mess you have made, God can clean it up. No matter how irredeemable it looks, God can redeem it. There is nothing in your life that is beyond Him. Nothing that He cannot restore, redeem, or make new. Nothing too small and nothing too big.

Two months after Joe and I got married, we conceived our

first baby boy, Judah. Thirteen months after that, we conceived our second baby boy, Nehemiah. And thirteen months after that, we conceived our third baby boy, Gideon. Three babies in four years!

We are just getting started, and I feel like I could already write a whole other book on God meeting us in the midst of marriage and parenthood, but we'll save that for a later date. In a nutshell, marriage and parenting are the most stretching, yet most rewarding things I have ever done in my entire life.

But I wouldn't have it any other way. Life with Jesus is everything. Joe and I are about to celebrate seven years of marriage. He's my person who I get to laugh with, cry with, and run after the Lord with. Our passion is and always will be Jesus. We hope and pray to one day be in full-time occupational ministry. In the meantime, we pursue to live our lives as full-time ministers right now. Ministering to the Lord, each other, and our boys is our first priority. And from that place, we live to minister to the world, giving away the love and Gospel of God to every person that we know and meet. We walk with Jesus every day, dreaming with Him and thanking Him for the wonderful life He has blessed us with.

Thinking about the way God has written His incredible story throughout my life, I'm in awe of how He does the same for all of His children. It's amazing to see His hand in every season, shaping us in ways we don't always expect and blessing us beyond our wildest dreams. He has far better plans in store for us than anything we could have ever come up with on our own.

# CHAPTER 24
# MEMORIAL STONES

"The past is a place of reference, not a place of residence."
Roy T. Bennett

I n the pages of this book, I've shared some of the precious jewels of my personal life stories. A "memorial stone" place is what I like to call certain seasons and chapters of my story. These are those monumental times or places in life where we feel the need to place a "stone" as a sort of bookmark that will never be removed. They mark certain spots, holding the place of particular pages in the books of our lives, specific chapters that we wanted pinned forever. Like New Start Ministry, the Evangelical Institute of Biblical Training, or that time I backslid and my friends prayed me through the valley.

I shared my stories in hope that you, too, will reflect on the jewels of your own life story. I hope that you will see in a new way that God is the world's best Author. The story that He has written over your life is full of adventure and miracles. It's powerful. It's purposeful. And even though it may be laced with some deep, dark valleys, it's also laced with some beautiful and brilliant mountain tops.

God's Word is full of wonderful stories that testify to His promise-keeping character. One begins in Genesis 12 with Him promising Abraham that his descendants would inherit the land of Canaan. The Israelites end up in slavery in Egypt, but God uses Moses to lead them out in Exodus. After wandering in the wilderness for forty years because of their disobedience, they are finally ready to enter the Promised Land. Unfortunately, Moses never got to step foot into the Promised Land; he only saw it with his eyes before he passed away. Joshua is chosen to take over as leader, and in Joshua 3, God supernaturally parts the Jordan River so that the Israelites can cross over on dry ground.

In Joshua 4:19-24, God tells the Israelites to take twelve stones from the river and set them up at Gilgal, where they are to serve as a reminder of His faithfulness.

> *"On the tenth day of the first month the people went up from the Jordan and camped at Gilgal on the eastern border of Jericho. And Joshua set up at Gilgal the twelve stones they had taken out of the Jordan. He said to the Israelites, 'In the future when your descendants ask their parents, "What do these stones mean?" tell them, "Israel crossed the Jordan on dry ground." For the LORD your God dried up the Jordan before you until you had crossed over. The LORD your God did to the Jordan what he had done to the Red Sea when he dried it up before us until we had crossed over. He did this so that all the peoples of the earth might know that the hand of the LORD is powerful and so that you might always fear the LORD your God.'"*

The stones were multi-purposed.

First, they served as a physical reminder of God's miraculous intervention. They were placed so that present and future generations might know and remember God. The stones would act as a conversation starter. When children would ask, "What do these stones mean?" parents would have an opportunity to recall and testify of God's faithfulness to them.

God constantly tells the Israelites in the Old Testament, *"Remember* the Lord your God." Remember and do not forget. I believe that remembering God and the things He has done in our lives is one way to keep ourselves humble and full of thanksgiving. It reminds us of who He is, what He's done, and that we are fully dependent on Him. And how can we remember such a great God, who has done such great things, without being filled with humility and thankfulness?

Secondly, the stones served as a symbol of unity among the twelve tribes of Israel. By taking one stone from each tribe, they were reminded of their collective identity as God's chosen people, all equally a part of His covenant promise.

Finally, the stones represented a marker of transition and spiritual renewal. They marked the Israelites' entrance into the Promised Land, signaling the end of their wilderness journey and the beginning of a new chapter in their history.

As we see how those memorial stones served purpose and held such symbolic weight, I pray this helps you to see the purpose and importance of your own memorial stones.

Even now, I encourage you to "Selah," as David says in the Psalms. Take an intentional pause in God's presence and reflect on how good God has been through every page of your own story. Invite the Holy Spirit to show you where He was in every moment of your life, even the ones that felt like He was nowhere to be found. As you reflect, you may want to write these moments down and find a bible verse that reminds you of where God had you in that moment. What was going on in your heart in that moment and how did God meet you? This is the act of selecting memorial stones from our own stories.

As you do so, I pray you're blessed to see that He has been right there with you all along.

Life in Christ is more than I could've ever imagined it to be. I cannot go back to the way things used to be. I can only go forward in Him. Luke 9:62 says, *"No one who puts a hand to the plow and looks back is fit for service in the kingdom of God."* This doesn't mean that we don't remember our past; it means that we don't long to return to our past. There's a difference between looking back with gratitude and looking back with regret. When you look back at your past, do you look back and say, "Thank You, God, that I'm not where I used to be?" Or do you look back and say, "Man, I miss where I used to be." Your past is meant for the occasional visit, not to set up camp and settle down there. Don't look back with regret, unless you want to go that way.

It is a beautiful and powerful thing to remember the Lord and all that He has done. When we look back, may we be like Joshua and the twelve tribes gathering stones, identifying the finger of God in our story and looking forward, beyond the river, into the Promised Land.

I pray that I never forget the places God has brought me from and that you never forget where He has brought you from either. May you never become comfortable with the simple Gospel, and may your own testimony never become too familiar to you. Always remember the Lord and those certain monumental times and places in your life that you feel are bookmark-worthy pages in your story.

# CHAPTER 25
## YOUR STORY MATTERS

*For I am not ashamed of the gospel, because it is the power of God
that brings salvation to everyone who believes:
first to the Jew, then to the Gentile.*
- Romans 1:16

The heart behind this book is for you to see my life laid bare before you. Some of these pages are filled with my gritty, grimy, dirty laundry blowing in the wind and hung out for you to see. For you to see that I have not been perfect, I am still a work in progress, and I have done some really horrible, bad, desperate, and disturbing things … *but God.* You see, our stories are not so much about what *we* have done, but rather about what *He* has done.

In Hebrew, the root of the word *testimony* means to duplicate, repeat, or do again. That means that when we share our stories, when we testify to what God has done in our lives, we are essentially saying, "God, do it again." Do it again in my spouse. Do it again in my parent. Do it again in my neighbor. Do it again in my friend. Do it again in my sibling. Do it again in a people group. Do it again in a generation. God does not show favoritism. What He has done in us, He wants to do again. That's why testimony is so important. Our testimony and the testimony of Jesus working in our lives imparts hope to others. When people hear that God did it for us, they can grab hold of hope, and their lives can change too.

There are stories in your belly, memories in your mind, treasures locked away in your heart that the world needs to hear. You have your own story to tell, and your story matters. Your story has the power to change someone else's life. That's why it's so important we walk in boldness, sharing with others where we've come from, what God has brought us through, and how He has done an amazing work, forever changing our lives for the best. How will our family, friends, coworkers, and people in our world know our story unless we tell them?

Sometimes people ask me, "Why do you share *that* part of your story? Aren't you scared of what people will think about you?"

And the answer is "no." I don't care what people think about who I was, because I'm not that person anymore. I share my story so freely, because I'm retelling the story of someone who has died. The old Miriah is dead. A new Miriah has been born. Born again in Jesus. That's why I share my story unashamed, because God gets all the glory. I'm not ashamed of the Gospel, because it is the power of God that brings salvation to everyone who believes.

You may think, "But what if they judge me?" And to that I say, "Are they your judge?"

You may think, "But what if they are ashamed of me?" I say, "Is Jesus ashamed of you?"

You may think, "But what if they look at me differently?" I say, "How does Jesus look at you?"

Instead of asking yourself, "What will they think of me," ask yourself, "What will they think of what God has done in me?"

Remember, your story is more about what *God* has done than it is about what *you* have done.

When you die to this world and hide your life in Jesus, then He can live through you. It's going to cost you everything. But when you count the cost and you say, "I'm willing to pay the price. I'm willing to be misunderstood. I'm willing to be talked bad about. I'm willing to be looked down upon. I'm willing to be humble. I'm willing to give it all," then you will freely give away all that God has given to you.

Be free from the opinion of others. Be free from the bondage of the past. You are not the person you used to be. You are who God says you are. When you share your story, remember who He says you are, then share from that place of freedom, humility, and knowing you are loved by God. When you share in this way, you will empower people around you to walk in freedom, humility, and knowing that they, too, are loved by God.

Still nervous about exposing your past? What if your story is the key that can unlock someone else's prison? Because sure, our stories are about us, but they're not only about us. Our stories are about Jesus. Him finding us, meeting us, healing us, helping us, and loving us. Your story could be exactly what the person in front of you needs to hear to change the course of their life. Your story could lead to their salvation. Your story could lead to their healing. Your story could help them in so many ways.

Someone else needs to hear how hard it has been. Someone else needs to know that they can make it out because you made it out. Someone else needs to know that they can change because you changed. Someone else needs to know that they can overcome depression because you overcame depression. Someone else needs to know that they can heal from past trauma, because you healed from past trauma. Someone else needs to know that they can quit doing drugs, because you quit doing drugs. Someone else needs to know that they can forgive when it hurts, because you forgave when it hurt. Someone else needs to know.

Stop thinking that your story is too boring or too small or too insignificant. Or maybe you think that your story is too extreme and too big and too much. Both are lies. Your story is your story. We humans love stories. And yours needs to be heard.

One way to share your story unashamedly is to make big of your weakness but to make even bigger of God's greatness. Share your dark times but share more of His light shining in those dark times. Tell them of how you fell but tell them more of how He picked you up. When your focus is on giving God the glory and making Him known, you will care less about what people think of you and more about what they think of Him. All is for His glory.

Storytelling is a universal human experience across every generation and culture. It is one of the oldest and most treasured traditions of humanity. One of the earliest forms of storytelling was through visual stories, like cave drawings. And then we have oral storytelling, which was the main method of preserving and passing along history for centuries. That is, until written languages came along and moved us into written stories. Stories were meant to be shared.[1]

Storytelling shapes our understanding of the world around us and has the ability to make lasting impact in our lives. While traditional books still remain a popular form of storytelling, this craft continues to evolve. Today we find ourselves in a digital era where stories are more accessible than ever. From eBooks and audio books to short, visual snippets on social media platforms like Instagram and TikTok to in-depth podcasts and YouTube videos, TV shows on streaming services, and personal blogs or online articles, the platforms for storytelling are seemingly endless.[2]

Therefore, we must remember our stories, recount them, recite them, and keep them alive. So, share yours, even if your voice shakes. Share even if you have tears in your eyes. Share knowing that if you *"Open wide your mouth [God] will fill it"* (Psalm 81:10). If you have a fear of public speaking or sharing your story, do it afraid. Do it by faith. Don't wait for the fear to leave you. Step out in the midst of the fear, trusting that God will meet you. God will give you the right words at the right time (See Matthew 10:19).

So, what does sharing your story look like for you personally? Will you write a book like I did? Share it through social media posts? Plan a coffee date with a friend or family member? Will you start a blog? Reach out to your local crisis pregnancy center or addiction recovery home? Will you invite your neighbor over for dinner or take your coworker out to lunch? Will you serve the inmates at your county jail or the homeless at your local soup kitchen? Will you share at women's ministry events or with the young people in your church youth group? What if the cashier at your favorite grocery store needs to hear your story? There are so many opportunities awaiting you!

At first, it may be a little uncomfortable; being vulnerable often is. But the more that you share, the easier it will get. Share as you feel led by the Holy Spirit, when you feel led by the Holy Spirit. I'm not saying you should share your entire story with every single person you meet, and you don't have to disclose every detail of what you have done or experienced. Use wisdom. But don't let fear or shame hold you back from testifying to what God has done in your life. Give Him His glory. Tell of His goodness. Speak the name of Jesus. Share your story ... without shame.

One final thing before we finish. Remember that every person you will ever meet also has their own story unique to who they are, where they've been, and what they've walked through. Ask them about their story as you share yours. You never know. God may use something they share to bless your heart in a way you didn't even know you needed. Their story may change your life.

# PROMPTS TO HELP YOU
# BEGIN SHARING YOUR STORY

**Sit with Jesus daily**. Everything you do and say should flow from your relationship with God. The more you plant yourself in God's word and allow God to heal you, the more freely you will share your story with others. *"**Heal** so that you don't bleed on people who didn't cut you."*

**Pray** and ask God to open doors for you to share your story. This may not be from a stage or a platform, but it may be with your neighbor, your waitress, or a family member. Ask God to open doors, then walk through the doors that He opens. Ask the Holy Spirit what specific details to share with whom.

**Know your story**. Spend time going over your story in your own mind so that you can clearly and accurately communicate the details and the timelines.

**Work to be able to share your testimony in 3-5 minutes or less.** I call this your "short form story." You won't always have an hour to sit down and talk to someone, but sometimes all someone needs to hear is a couple pages from your book, not the entire thing. Write it on an index card or in your journal. You can use the questions below as a simple outline.

1.      Who was I?

2.      What did God do?

3.      Who am I now?

**Practice** sharing your story first with people you trust. Ask your spouse or a friend or family member if they will listen to you share your "short form story" for a few minutes. Even reciting it out loud to yourself in the mirror can help you get more comfortable sharing. Just be yourself. Don't overthink it.

Always **share with God and others in mind**. Remember that sharing your story with others is for the purpose of encouraging them and glorifying God. Never share from a self-centered place. People can see right through fakery, and they crave authenticity and vulnerability.

**Have fun**! Even when recounting the painful and hard parts of your story, remember that the goal is helping others and glorifying God. It's fun to see peoples' eyes light up when they realize they're not alone or that you would trust them enough to share a special part of your heart with them. Have fun doing it.

*You too can tell your story without shame and live an unashamed life.*

# MY PRAYER FOR YOU

God, You see and know the one reading this book. You see and know every detail of their story, even the details they may have forgotten. Every single one of their days has been written in Your book. You know every hair on their head. You are acquainted with every part of who they are, and You know every thought in their mind. I pray, Lord, that right now You open their eyes wide to the depths of Your love for them, because Your love changes everything. I pray that You touch them by the power of Your Holy Spirit right now and that You fill them with Your Spirit, Your fire, and Your boldness. Let Your Word and the testimony of what You have done become like a fire in their bones that they must release to the world around them. Let them burn for the lost, the hurting, the overlooked, and the sinner.

I bless you right now with courage to share your story. I pray that as you look to the Lord, your face will never again be covered with shame. I command every accusing voice to be silent, in the name of Jesus. I command all condemnation to be broken off of your life. Every voice that says that you are less than or unimportant, be silent in the name of Jesus. Every voice that says that you are too much or too loud, be silent in the name of Jesus. I pray that you dive into God's word. And God, I ask

You to fill them now with a deep hunger for You and Your Word, so that when they share their story with others, it is laced with truth and healing, not trauma and hurt.

Bless you, be healed, be free, be unashamed. In the mighty name of Jesus.

With love,
Miriah

# NOTES

## 1. THE CHOICE IS YOURS

1. Krockow, Eva M., Ph.D., "How Many Decisions Do We Make Each Day?" Psychology Today, September 27, 2018, https://www.psychologytoday.com/us/blog/stretching-theory/201809/how-many-decisions-do-we-make-each-day.

## 4. TRUE LOVE DOES (NOT) EXIST

1. "What You Need to Know about Youth Suicide," NAMI, Accessed November 13, 2024, https://www.psychologytoday.com/us/blog/stretching-theory/201809/how-many-decisions-do-we-make-each-day.

## 5. THE GATEWAY DRUG

1. Frysh, Paul. Medically Reviewed by Jabeen Begum, MD. "How Pot Affects Your Mind and Body." WebMD. January 12, 2024. https://www.webmd.com/mental-health/addiction/marijuana-use-and-its-effects.
2. Feldscher, Karen, "What Led to the Opiod Crisis-and How to Fix It," Harvard T.H. Chan, February 9, 2022, https://hsph.harvard.edu/news/what-led-to-the-opioid-crisis-and-how-to-fix-it/.

## 6. ALL I NEED IN THIS LIFE OF SIN IS ME AND MY GIRLFRIEND

1. Bevere, Lisa, "True Love Speaks: Why We Can't Stay Silent In a Culture of Confusion," Moral Revolution, June 30, 2020, https://moralrevolution.com/true-love-speaks-why-we-cant-stay-silent-in-a-culture-of-confusion/.

## 10. HIGH SCHOOL AND HANGOVERS

1. "What Are the Harms?" Rethinking Drinking: Alcohol and Your Health, National Institute of Alcohol Abuse and Alcoholism, Accessed February 17, 2025, https://rethinkingdrinking.niaaa.nih.gov/how-much-too-much/what-are-harms.

## 11. CHASING THE DRAGON

1. "How Meth Destroys the Body," FRONTLINE, PBS, February 14, 2006, Updated May 17, 2011, https://www.pbs.org/wgbh/pages/frontline/meth/body/.

## 12. GET-OUT-OF-JAIL FREE CARD

1. Alcoholics Anonymous. "The Start and Growth of A.A." Accessed December 11, 2024. https://www.aa.org/the-start-and-growth-of-aa.
2. Wikipedia. "Narcotics Anonymous." Accessed December 11, 2024. https://en.wikipedia.org/wiki/Narcotics_Anonymous.
3. Greater Philadelphia Region of Narcotics Anonymous. "The Twelve Traditions of NA." Accessed December 11, 2024. https://naworks.org/readings/traditions/.

## 16. A BROKEN HALLELUJAH

1. DeMarco, Michele, Ph.D., Rev, "The 'Write' Way to Heal: Ten practices for transforming emotional pain and re-authoring your life," Psychology Today, Updated November 12, 2023, https://www.psychologytoday.com/us/blog/soul-console/202311/the-write-way-to-heal.

## 25. YOUR STORY MATTERS

1. "Storytelling," National Geographic Education, Accessed March 10, 2025, https://education.nationalgeographic.org/resource/storytelling-x/.
2. Admin, "Oral Storytelling Traditions and Appalachian Storytelling: From Ancient Practices to Today's Revival," John C. Campbell Folk School, October 15, 2023, https://www.folkschool.org/2023/10/15/the-history-and-art-of-storytelling/.

# ACKNOWLEDGMENTS

To my mom, Cathy and my dad, David who raised me the best they could and instilled biblical nuggets of truths in me over the years. That was the best thing you guys could have ever done for me. Thank you. I love you.

To my sister, Sydney and my brother, Holden who never stopped loving me even in the darkness and lowest moments of my life. Thank you. I love you both.

To the countless people who prayed for me to come to Christ and to all the strangers who were bold enough to sow seeds of truth into my life over the years. Thank you. God was faithful to bring the increase.

To my wonderful husband Joe, who pushed me to write this book and who encourages me and points me to Jesus every single day. I couldn't have finished it without you, seriously. Thank you, Baby. I love you.

And lastly, to Michael Cline. I'm not sure I would have ever surrendered to Jesus if I had never met you. Loving you changed everything! Thank you.

# ABOUT THE AUTHOR

Miriah Taverna has been married to her best friend, Joe, for seven years, and they have three awesome little boys. She enjoys thrifting, reading Christian books, good coffee, hiking with her boys, and beating Joe in Super Mario Kart!

After six years in addiction, multiple rehabs, drug classes, and even jail, Miriah still wouldn't stop using. But in 2013, she had a radical encounter with the love and power of God that completely changed her life. Once bound by confusion, depression, addiction, and sexual sin, she is now a living testimony of God's grace and mercy. Her greatest desire is to make Jesus known and see others set free, just as she was.

Miriah holds degrees in Biblical Studies, Biblical Exposition, and Church Ministry. She and Joe have served as youth pastors and home group leaders. She shares her story at addiction recovery groups, youth groups, women's gatherings, and anywhere God opens the door. She believes the world is our mission field and that every moment can be a divine moment.

Miriah's heart burns for the next generation. She uses social media to reach people with raw authenticity, bold faith, and the uncompromising truth of God's Word. She speaks the truth in love, especially in a culture that often trades truth for comfort. Through her videos, writing, and everyday conversations, she invites others into the abundant life that only Jesus can offer.

More than anything, Miriah longs to see people walk in purity, purpose, and boldness, unashamed of the Gospel. Whether through her book, online content, or personal encouragement, her message remains the same: Jesus loves you. Jesus saves. Jesus has a beautiful plan for your life.

Miriah's story is proof that God will meet you right where you are—but He won't leave you there. Through every word she writes or speaks, her prayer is that you won't just hear her voice —but that you'll hear His.

To learn more about Miriah and her ministry,
visit https://www.miriahtaverna.com/.

You can also find her here:

youtube.com/@miriahtaverna
tiktok.com/@miriahtaverna
instagram.com/miriahtaverna
facebook.com/miriahataverna